*Radio Times* **BOOK OF**

# SPORTING
# DATES

## About the Author

Ian Morrison was born in Liverpool but now spends most of his time on the Mediterranean isle of Mallorca. A full-time freelance author since 1983 this is his 80th book on a wide variety of sports, many of which have been of an encyclopedia nature and have proved to be a great help to him in compiling the *Radio Times Book of Sporting Dates.*

# *RadioTimes* BOOK OF
# SPORTING
# DATES

## IAN MORRISON

## Acknowledgements

The author would like to thank, as always, his wife Ann for her help with the proof reading ... although she cannot complain this time because she got a good suntan in the process!

Network Books is an imprint of BBC Books,
a division of BBC Enterprises Limited,
Woodlands, 80 Wood Lane,
London W12 0TT

First published 1993

ISBN 0 563 36959 0

Illustrations by David Downton

Set in Monophoto Calisto and Gill by Selwood Systems, Midsomer Norton
Printed and bound in Great Britain by Butler & Tanner Ltd, Frome
Cover printed by Clays Ltd, St Ives Plc

# CONTENTS

Introduction   6

January   7

February   27

March   45

April   69

May   89

June   111

July   131

August   153

September   173

October   193

November   215

December   235

## Introduction

Welcome to the *Radio Times Book of Sporting Dates* which is a must for all armchair sporting fans. No matter what your sporting interest, you will be able to refer to any date of the year and find out what happened on that date. With over one thousand entries on more than 30 popular sports there is bound to be something to arouse your sporting interest. It is ideal for checking forthcoming sporting anniversaries and, of course, is a welcome addition to any quiz 'buff's library.

# JANUARY

# JANUARY

**1**

**Baron Pierre de Coubertin,** founder of the Modern Olympic Games, was born in **1863**. A keen all-round sportsman, he was also a top-class rugby referee and in 1906 took charge of France's first international on home soil ... **Football goal nets** were used for the first time in a senior match at Bolton in **1890** ... In **1910 France was beaten 49–14** (59–16 on present-day scoring) by Wales at Swansea, the biggest win in the rugby union international championship; William Bancroft kicked a record nine goals for Wales ... When **Sunderland and Aston Villa** met at Roker Park on this day in **1953** they became the first two Football League clubs to play each other for the 100th time in the League; the teams drew 2–2 ... In the **1965** honours list, **Stanley Matthews** became the first footballer to receive a knighthood ... In **1989 Eric Bristow** became the first darts player to receive an honour—the MBE.

**2**

In **1930 Jim Dyet** of King's Park scored eight goals against Forfar in a Scottish League second-division match. It was Dyet's League debut, and a British League record! ... At Twickenham in **1936, Alexander Obolensky,** the son of a Russian prince, scored one of the finest tries ever witnessed at the ground when he raced 50 yards (46 m) diagonally across the pitch. Obolensky scored two tries in the 13–0 win against the All Blacks, which became known as 'Obolensky's Match' ... Back in Scotland, in **1939,** a crowd of 118,567 watched Rangers play Celtic, **the biggest gate for a soccer League game in Britain** ... The corresponding fixture at Ibrox Stadium in **1971** produced **one of the worst disasters in British sporting history.** A barrier collapsed, killing 66 spectators and injuring 145, when thousands of Rangers fans leaving the ground returned to share the elation of a late equalizer by Colin Stein.

**3** One of America's top sportsmen, ice-hockey player **Bobby Hull,** was born in **1939.** Twice winner of the coveted Hart Trophy, he scored 610 goals in the NHL and in his 1600th game in 1978 he scored his 1000th point. No man has scored 1000 points in so few games ... Scottish rugby union international **Gavin Hastings** was born on this day in **1962.** He has scored more points than any other British player, with more than 400 to his credit ... In American Football, **Tony Dorsett** ran an NFL record 99 yards (90m) from a scrimmage while playing for Dallas Cowboys against the Minnesota Vikings in **1983** ... Playing for Manchester United against Southampton in **1987, Liam O'Brien** was sent off after just 85 seconds, the quickest dismissal in the first division (now Premier League) ... In **1992, Martin Offiah** became the most valuable player in rugby league history when he joined Wigan from Widnes for a world record £440,000.

**4** Former world heavyweight boxing champion **Floyd Patterson** was born in **1935.** The Olympic middleweight champion of 1952, Patterson defeated Archie Moore in 1956 for the heavyweight title left vacant by Rocky Marciano's retirement, becoming the youngest holder of the title. Patterson lost his title to Ingemar Johansson in 1959, but defeated the Swede a year later to become the first man to regain the title ... New Zealand squash champion **Susan Devoy** was born on this day in **1964.**

World champion four times, she also won the British Open title seven years in succession, 1984–90 ... In **1967 Donald Campbell,** son of Sir Malcolm Campbell, died on Coniston Water in the Lake District while attempting to break the world water speed record in *Bluebird.* His ageing craft somersaulted after hitting the wake from the first run (*see 11 March*) ... The **1982** England v Australia rugby international at Twickenham got more publicity than it bargained for when the well-endowed **Erika Roe** made her 'debut', much to the delight of the packed crowd and millions more watching on television ... In **1991** 12-year-old **Fu Mingxia** of China won the women's world platform diving title to become the youngest world champion in any sport.

**5**

The former Manchester United footballer **Bill Foulkes** was born this day in **1932**. He was a member of the team that beat Portuguese club Benfica in the final of the 1968 European Champions' Cup. Also playing that day, for Benfica, was **Eusébio**, who was born on the same day but in **1943**. European Footballer of the Year in 1965 and the man behind Portugal's rise to the top of world football in the 1960s, he helped to establish Benfica as one of the best clubs in Europe. He collected a European Champions' Cup winners' medal in 1962, but was three times on the losing side ... The body of former world heavyweight boxing champion **Sonny Liston** was found in a Las Vegas apartment in **1971** ... On the same day in **1971, Australia and England** met in the first one-day cricket international at Melbourne.

**6** In **1930** cricketer **Don Bradman** scored a world record 452 not out while playing for New South Wales against Queensland. His innings surpassed Bill Ponsford's old record of 437 runs . . . **Stockport County beat Halifax Town 13–0** in a third-division (north) game in **1934.** It remains the biggest winning margin in Football League history (*see 5 October*) . . . One of soccer's greatest managers, **Herbert Chapman**, died this day in **1934.** He guided both Huddersfield and Arsenal to a hat-trick apiece of League championships in the 1920s and 30s . . . Several well-known sports personalities share this birth date; former Tottenham Hotspur chief executive **Terry Venables** was born in **1943.** Venables is the only player to have represented England at every level. He played at Schoolboy, Youth, Amateur, Under-23 (now Under-21) and Full International. He was also a co-writer of the 1970s TV detective series *Hazel* . . . Former Welsh rugby international **Barry John** was born in **1945.** He scored 188 points in Australia and New Zealand in 1971, a British Lions tour record. . . . Indian cricketer **Kapil Dev** was born in **1959.** This great all-rounder captained his country to victory in the 1982 World Cup.

**7** One of the world's best known basketball teams, the **Harlem Globetrotters,** was founded by Abraham Saperstein of Chicago in **1927.** A touring team renowned as much for their comedy routines and showmanship as their undoubted technical skills, they are always greeted on court by their theme tune, *Sweet Georgia Brown.* One of their best-known players was Meadowlark Lemmon . . . The most prolific world record breaker in sporting history was born on this day in **1942:**

Russian weightlifter **Vasily Alexeev,** who set 80 official world records. He won eight world and Olympic titles between 1970 and 1977. For breakfast he used to eat a 36-egg omelette! . . . In **1972** the **Los Angeles Lakers** won their 33rd consecutive game in the National Basketball Association (NBA). The Lakers ended the season with a record 69 wins and only 13 defeats and went on to beat the New York Knicks 4–1 to win the NBA title.

**8** Boxer **Frank Erne** was born in **1875.** Erne proudly stands as the only Swiss-born boxer ever to hold a world title, becoming lightweight champion in 1899 by beating 'Kid' Lavigne. He unsuccessfully challenged for the featherweight and welterweight titles . . . **Calvin Smith,** once the fastest man on earth, was born in **1961.** Smith broke the world 100 metres record at Colorado Springs in 1983. Shortly afterwards he captured the 200 metres gold medal at the inaugural world championships in Helsinki, but could only manage silver in the 100 metres. He retained his 200 metres title in Rome four years later. The boycott of 1980 prevented his chance of Olympic gold . . . The **Los Angeles Raiders** won their first American Football Conference (AFC) Championship in **1984** by beating Seattle 30–14. They went on to win Super Bowl XVIII by beating the Washington Redskins . . . 8 January **1990** is a day **Cardiff City FC** will want to forget. An FA Cup tie with QPR gave the club its biggest pay-day for years—until thieves broke in and helped themselves to over £50,000 in takings.

**9** In **1811** the **first recorded golf tournament for women** took place, at Musselburgh. In a commendably non-chauvinistic gesture for the early nineteenth century, the local golf club agreed to put up a prize of a creel (fishing basket) to be contested by the fishwives of the area. As the women did the same work as their male counterparts, the club felt that the sporting activities enjoyed by the men should also be open to them. The fishwives already played an annual Shrove Tuesday football match, so there was no reason to exclude them from the golf links ... At New York's Madison Square Garden in **1942 Joe Louis** successfully defended his world heavyweight title for the twentieth time when he knocked out Buddy Baer, brother of Max, four seconds from the end of the first round. In their previous encounter, a year earlier, Baer had become the first man to be disqualified in a world heavyweight title fight. Buddy's nephew, Max Baer junior, played the part of Jethro in the popular television series *The Beverly Hillbillies.*

**10**

In **1920** the **Montreal Canadiens** ice hockey team beat Toronto St Patricks 14–7. The 21 goals established a new National Hockey League (NHL) record, beating the 19 scored in 1917, when the Montreal Wanderers beat the Toronto Arenas 10–9 ... **New Zealand** played their first Test match this day in **1930** when they entertained England at Lancaster Park, Christchurch. The England Team was weakened by the absence of some established players who were making up a second Test side simultaneously touring in the West Indies. Nevertheless, England won the match by eight wickets, with Maurice Allom's 5 wickets for 38 runs decisive ... At Bombay in **1985 Ravi Shastri** emulated the feat of Gary Sobers 17 years earlier (*see 31 August*) when he hit six sixes in one over. Playing for Bombay,

Shastri's 36 runs came off the bowling of Tilak Raj of Baroda ... In **1991 Manchester United** announced that they were to follow Tottenham Hotspur's example and become a public company with shares quoted on the Stock Exchange.

## 11

The first of the great British jockeys, **Fred Archer,** was born in **1857.** He rode 2748 winners from 8084 mounts between 1870, when he was only 13, and 1886. He was champion jockey every year from 1874 to 1886. He won 21 Classic races, including the Derby five times (*see 4 and 8 November*) ... Another top racing man, trainer **Henry Cecil,** was also born on this day, in **1943.** He trained a record 180 winners on the flat in 1987 ... In **1959 Hanif Mohammad** completed the highest innings in first-class cricket when he scored 499 for Karachi against Bahawalpur at Karachi, surpassing Don Bradman's old record of 452 not out (*see 6 January*). Facing the last ball of the day, Hanif went for a quick single to notch up 500 but was run out! His mammoth total had taken 10 hours 35 minutes to compile. ... **Steve Davis** made history on this day in **1982** when, playing against John Spencer in the Lada Classic at Oldham, he recorded snooker's first televised maximum 147 break. Ironically, this distinction would have been Spencer's three years earlier, during the televised Holsten Lager Tournament at Slough, if the Thames TV cameramen had not been at lunch due to a union ruling! ... On this day in **1991 Chelsea** were fined a record £105,000 by the Football League for making irregular payments to players.

## 12

Rugby league international **Mike Sullivan** was born in **1934.** He scored a record 45 international tries between 1954 and

1963 ... Ex-world heavyweight boxing champion **Joe Frazier** was born in **1947.** He captured the New York version of the title in 1968 and became the unified champion in 1970 when he beat Jimmy Ellis. He beat Muhammad Ali in 1971, the first man to do so, but Ali gained revenge in the 'Thrilla in Manila' four years later ... In **1959 Henry Cooper** beat Brian London over 15 rounds to win his first British title.

**13** **Thomas Lord,** the man who founded the Lord's Cricket Ground, died in **1832** (*see 23 November*) ... American golfer **Mark O'Meara** was born in **1957.** While he has not won a Major, he has been a consistent money winner since joining the US Tour in 1981; in 1984 he was second on the money list. His career earnings have topped $4 million ... **Stephen Hendry,** the youngest man to win the Embassy world professional snooker title, was born in **1969.** He was only 21 years and 106 days when he first won the title in 1990, surpassing the 18-year-old record of Alex Higgins (*see 18 March*). In 1992 Hendry beat Jimmy White 18–14 in a remarkable turnaround, winning the last 10 frames, to take his second title. He won the title a third time in 1993, again at the expense of Jimmy White ... In **1974** the **Miami Dolphins** beat Minnesota Vikings 24–7 at Houston to win back-to-back Super Bowls ... The opposing goalkeepers in the Preston versus Bury Football League game on this day in **1990** were brothers **Alan and Gary Kelly.** Their father, Alan, was also a goalkeeper for Preston.

**14** Playing for Celtic against Dunfermline in a Scottish League first division game in **1928, Jimmy McGrory** scored a first/Premier division record eight goals. In the same season Owen McNally of Arthurlie had become the first man to score eight goals in a Scottish League game, against Armadale in the second division; over the next ten seasons Jim Dyet (King's Park), John Calder (Morton) and Norman Haywood (Raith Rovers) equalled the records set by McNally and McGrory. No man has since scored as many goals in a Scottish League game ... Australian golfer **Graham Marsh,** brother of Test cricketer Rodney Marsh, was born in **1944.** His finest moment was in 1977 when he beat Ray Floyd to win the World Match-Play Championship at Wentworth ... On this day in **1958** a crowd of 60,000 watched **Manchester United** beat Red Star Belgrade 2–1 in a European Cup tie at Old Trafford. The second leg three weeks later was to be the last appearance of the 'Busby Babes' before the Munich Air Disaster (*see 6 February*).

## 15

In **1927 BBC Radio gave its first live commentary of a rugby match**, Teddy Wakelam reporting on the first international from Twickenham between England and Wales. England won 11–9 ... Wellington batsman **John Reid** scored a world record 15 sixes in his innings of 296 against Northern Districts at Wellington in **1963** ... Playing in front of a 62,000 crowd at the Memorial Coliseum, Los Angeles, the Green Bay Packers beat Kansas City Chiefs 35–10 to win the **first Super Bowl** in **1967.** Max McGee and Elijah Pitts each scored two touchdowns for the victors, for whom Bart Starr became the first winner of the coveted Most Valuable Player (MVP) award ... Ukrainian pole-vaulter **Sergey Bubka** set his first world record, with a vault of 19 feet $\frac{1}{4}$ inch (5·81 m), in **1984** ... At

Bournemouth in **1985** snooker player **Stacey Hillyard** made history when she became the first woman to compile a century break in a competitive match. Hillyard, who was only 15 at the time, compiled 114 playing in a local league match ... At Madras in **1988**, Indian bowler **Narendra Hirwani** produced the best figures for a player on his Test match debut, taking 16 wickets for 136 runs against the West Indies. Bob Massie also took 16 wickets, but for 137 runs, on his debut for Australia against England at Lord's in 1972.

**16**

One of the best-known names on the American Indy Car circuit, **A. J. Foyt,** was born in **1935**. In 1977 he became the first man to win the Indianapolis 500 endurance race four times, having won it previously in 1961, 1964 and 1967. Al Unser senior and Rick Mears have since equalled Foyt's record ... Canadian snooker player **Cliff Thorburn** was born in **1948**. He captured a thrilling world title at the Crucible Theatre in 1980 when he beat Alex Higgins 18–16. He also made history in 1983 (*see 23 April*) when he became the first man to compile a maximum break in the world championship. In 1989, he became the first man to register two official maximum breaks in tournament play.

**17**

On this day in **1933** the MCC received a telegram from the Australian Cricket Board complaining about the **excessive use of 'bodyline' bowling by Harold Larwood** in the infamous Test series. The England pace bowler's tactic of aiming deliveries at the batsman's body sparked a fierce controversy and caused a lot of ill-feeling between the two nations (*see 14 November*) ...

One of the world's best-known sportsmen, boxer **Muhammad Ali,** was born in **1942.** As Cassius Clay he won the Olympic light-heavyweight title in 1960. This achievement is reputed to have meant so much to him that he kept the medal round his neck, even when in the bath, for weeks after winning the title! He turned professional shortly after his Olympic triumph and in Miami in 1964 (*see 25 February*) he caused a sensation by defeating the seemingly invincible Sonny Liston for the world heavyweight title. In the return bout he beat Liston with a first round knockout and defended his crown successfully in the ring until stripped of it by the authorities in 1967 for refusing to be drafted into the US Army. He regained the title in 1974, beating George Foreman, for a further four years before losing it to Leon Spinks. Seven months later he beat Spinks to become the first man to twice regain the title. He made an unsuccessful attempt to regain it a third time against Larry Holmes in 1980. Ali retired in 1982 following a points defeat by Trevor Berbick . . . The first-division match between **Manchester United and Arsenal** in **1948** drew a Football League record crowd of 83,260. The game was played at Manchester City's Maine Road ground because war damage had put Old Trafford out of action. The game ended 1–1.

# 18

**England beat Wales 2–1** at Kennington Oval in **1879** in the first soccer international between the two countries . . . National Hunt jockey **Richard Dunwoody** was born in **1964.** In the 1991–92 season he won a National Hunt record £923,974 in prize money. He rode West Tip to win the 1986 Grand National.

**19**

Great Britain rugby league coach **Mal Reilly** was born in **1948.** He spent his playing career with Castleford and Manly (Australia) before returning to 'Cas' as coach in 1974. As a player he won most of the game's top honours including two challenge cup winners' medals. In 1969 he won the Lance Todd Trophy ... Sweden's top lawn tennis player **Stefan Edberg** was born in **1966.** He captured the Wimbledon title in 1988 when he beat Boris Becker in four sets. The two contested the 1989 final which Becker won in straight sets. Edberg regained his title the following year after a five-set marathon. He won his first Grand Slam event in 1985 when he took the Australian title ... In the rugby union international championship of **1991 England** had their first win in Cardiff for 28 years. On the same day **Serge Blanco,** playing for France against Scotland, became the most capped rugby union player.

**20**

The **first game of basketball** was played at the YMCA Training School, Springfield, Massachusetts, in **1892.** The game had been devised a month previously by Dr James Naismith ... In **1974 Millwall and Fulham** met at The Den in the first Football League game to be played on a Sunday. Millwall won 1–0 with a goal by Brian Clark ... Swimmer **Johnny Weissmuller** died in **1984.** He was the first man to swim 100 metres in under one minute, in 1922. He won both the 100 and 400 metres freestyle gold medals at the 1924 Paris Olympics. He retained his 100 metres title in Amsterdam four years later. He also won gold in the relay at both Games. In 1928 he was a member of the US Water Polo team that took the bronze medal. When his swimming career ended, he went to Hollywood where he made, in 1934, the first of the 12 Tarzan movies that would keep him in the public eye. He was the first of four Olympic medallists to play the title role; the others were Buster Crabbe, Herman Brix and Glenn Morris (*see 2 June*).

## 21

The inaugural **Monte Carlo Rally,** one of the best-known long-distance motor races, got under way on this day in 1911 (*see 28 January*) ... **Jack Nicklaus,** the greatest golfer of the modern era, was born in 1940. A professional since 1961 he has won an all-time record 18 professional majors. His first major win was the US Open, in 1962. He has won this tournament four times, the PGA Championship five times, the British Open on three occasions and the US Masters a record six times; the last being in 1986 at the age of 46. The winner of over $5 million in prize-money, he has continued his winning ways since joining the Seniors' Tour in 1990.

## 22

Former Everton and England centre-forward **Dixie Dean** was born on this day in 1907. In 1927–28 he scored a record 60 goals in a Football League season. Dean died while watching a local Everton–Liverpool 'derby' in 1980 ... The man who guided England to World Cup glory in 1966, **Sir Alf Ramsey,** was born in 1920. He was appointed England manager in 1963, a year after taking Ipswich to the first division title ... Former world heavyweight boxing champion **George Foreman** was born in 1949. He won the title by beating Joe Frazier in 1973 and made two successful defences before losing to Muhammad Ali in Kinshasa, Zaïre, in 1974. He came out of retirement in the 1980s to have another crack at the world crown and in 1991,

at the age of 43, was beaten on points by Evander Holyfield ...
**Joe Davis** compiled the first official maximum snooker break
of 147 in **1955,** playing against Willie Smith at the Leicester
Square Hall ... Britain's first world motor-racing champion,
**Mike Hawthorn,** died in **1959** when the Jaguar he was driving
went out of control on the Guildford by-pass ... British
swimmer **Nick Gillingham,** the bronze medallist in the 200
metres breaststroke at the 1992 Barcelona Olympics, was born
in **1967**.

**23** The most successful manager in Football League history, **Bob
Paisley,** was born in **1919.** He joined Liverpool from Bishop
Auckland as a player in 1939 and stayed over 40 years with the
club. He took over from Bill Shankly in 1974 and went on
to lead the club through an unprecedented period of success,
capturing six League titles, the European Cup three times, the
Milk Cup three times, and the UEFA and European Super
Cups once each. He was manager of the year a record six
times—hardly surprisingly! (*see 7 February*) ... On this day in
**1958** Pakistan batsman **Hanif Mohammad,** the man responsible for the highest innings in first-class cricket, completed the
longest innings. He went to the crease against the West Indies
at Bridgetown, Barbados, on 20 January and stayed there for 16
hours 10 minutes, scoring a massive 337 runs.

**24** The **BBC televised its first steeplechase** in **1948,** from
Sandown Park ... In **1982** the **San Francisco 49ers** beat the
Cincinnati Bengals 26–21 to win Super Bowl XVI. It was the first
of a record-equalling four wins for the 49ers, who dominated the

gridiron game in the United States in the 1980s. They won their second title in 1985, easily beating the Dolphins 38–16, their third in 1989 when they beat the Bengals 20–16, and the following year set a Super Bowl record by trouncing the Denver Broncos 55–10. Their quarterback, Joe Montana, won the MVP Award in 1982, 1985 and 1990, becoming the first man to win three Super Bowl MVP awards ... Yugoslav tennis player **Monica Seles** won her second successive Australian Open title in **1992** when she beat Mary-Jo Fernandez of the US 6–2, 6–3. A year earlier she had defeated Jana Novotna 5–7, 6–3, 6–1 to become, at 17, the youngest-ever Australian women's champion.

## 25

**Lord Lonsdale,** the president of the National Sporting Club, who lends his name to the most coveted trophy in British boxing, the Lonsdale Belt, was born in **1857.** His belts, which were inaugurated in 1909, become the permanent property of any boxer who wins three British title fights in a weight division. The first person to win one outright was featherweight Jim Driscoll, in January 1911 ... On this day in **1895 Wales** lost 3–0 to Ireland at Rhyl in the first international hockey match ... The **first Winter Olympics** got under way at Chamonix, France, in **1924.** A total of 281 men and 13 women from 16 countries took part ... Spanish motor cyclist **Angel Nieto** was born in **1947.** He won seven world 125cc and six 50cc titles. His total of 13 titles is just two short of the record set by Giacomo Agostini. Nieto's total of 90 race wins has also only been bettered by the brilliant Agostini ... In **1992,** Britain's **Steve Backley** became the first man to throw the modified javelin 300 feet (91 m) at a meeting at Auckland, New Zealand.

**26** The first meeting of the **Rugby Football Union** at the Pall Mall Restaurant, near Trafalgar Square, in 1871 was attended by representatives from 21 clubs and schools ... Golfer **Henry Cotton** was born in 1907. He was the last Briton before Nick Faldo to win the British Open three times and was the only golfer to win the title both before and after the Second World War. His second-round 65 during his first Open win at Sandwich in 1934 was one of the finest seen in the championship and remained a record for a single round for over 40 years. He also won the title in 1937 and 1948, at Carnoustie and Muirfield respectively ... Probably the greatest, and certainly highest paid, ice hockey player of all-time, **Wayne Gretzky,** was born in 1961. Nine times winner of the National Hockey league (NHL) MVP Award, he led Edmonton to four Stanley Cups, 1984–88, and is the all-time top points scorer in the NHL ... **West Indies beat Australia** by one run in the Fourth Test at Adelaide in 1993, the narrowest winning margin in Test Cricket history.

**27** On this day in 1913 American athlete **Jim Thorpe** was stripped of his Olympic medals after it was discovered he had been paid for playing baseball a couple of years earlier. Of mixed Irish/French/Red Indian descent, Thorpe was an outstanding footballer and baseball player. He was also a keen athlete and was selected for the 1912 Stockholm Olympics. He won the pentathlon and decathlon gold medals and finished fourth in the high jump and seventh in the long jump. He returned to the United States a national hero, but the following January it was revealed he had received $25 for playing minor league baseball in 1909 and 1910. He was stripped of his medals. Thorpe enjoyed successful careers in professional baseball and gridiron before dying suddenly at the age of 64 in 1953. In January 1983 thirty years after his family made moves to have Jim Thorpe's name reinstated in the record books, his gold medals were presented to his children ... In Superbowl XXV in **1991** the **New York Giants beat the Buffalo Bills 20–19** to record the closest Superbowl win in history.

**28**

The first **Monte Carlo Rally** ended in **1911** with Frenchman Henri Rougier, in a Turcat-Mery, declared the winner. Sandro Munari (Italy) and Walter Röhrl (Germany) have each won this famous race a record four times. The most successful manufacturer has been Lancia, with 12 wins ... South African golfer **Nick Price** was born in **1957** ... At the Louisiana Superdrome, New Orleans, in **1990,** the **San Francisco 49ers beat the Denver Broncos 55–10** in the most one-sided, and highest scoring, Super Bowl. The 49ers led 13–3 at the end of the first quarter, were 27–3 up at half time, and were 41–7 in front with one quarter remaining. Jerry Rice scored three touchdowns for a record-equalling 18 points in a Super Bowl. Mike Cofer kicked a record seven 'points after'.

**29**

South African motor-racing driver **Jody Scheckter** was born in **1950.** He started his formula one career with Tyrrell and then partnered the new Wolf car to its first success in the opening race of the 1977 season, in Argentina. Two years later, now with Ferrari, Scheckter became the first and only South African to lift the world championship, with wins in the Belgian, Italian and Monaco grands prix. Twelve months after lifting the world crown, and with a career total of 11 grand prix wins from 112 starts, he announced his retirement.

**30** In **1911** Welshman **Jim Driscoll,** nicknamed 'peerless Jim', became the first man to win a Lonsdale Belt outright (*see 25 January*) when he stopped 'Spike' Robson in the 11th round of their British featherweight title fight in London ... Former chess supremo **Boris Spassky** was born in **1938.** He succeeded Tigran Petrosian as world champion in 1969, but lost his title to the American Bobby Fischer in a much publicized match at Reykjavik, Iceland, in 1972. The rematch in 1992 again attracted a lot of publicity ... A couple of top American golfers share birthdays this day. **Curtis Strange,** the top US money-winner in 1985, 1987 and 1988, was born in **1955.** A professional since 1976, he earned himself a place in the record books in 1989 when he became the first man since Ben Hogan, in 1951, to win the US Open in consecutive years ... The other birthday boy, **Payne Stewart,** is easily identified on the golf course by virtue of his plus 'twos', bright clothing and the logos he wears for the National Football League (NFL) with whom he enjoys a unique sponsorship contract. Born in **1957,** Stewart turned professional in 1979. His consistency throughout the 1980s was rewarded in 1989 by victory in the PGA championship, his first Major, after coming close so many times. Two years later he won the US Open.

**31** Athlete **Chris Chataway** was born in **1931.** He was in the field when Roger Bannister became the first man to run a mile in under four minutes at Oxford in 1954. He won the gold medal in the three miles at that year's Empire and Commonwealth Games and in 1954–55 broke three world records, at three miles and 5000 metres. He quit athletics in 1956 and later became an MP and Cabinet Minister ... Top baseball player **Nolan Ryan,** probably the fastest pitcher the game has seen, was born in **1947.** In 1974 one of his deliveries was clocked at over 100 mph (160 km/h). Not surprisingly, his career has yielded an all-time record of more than 5600 strikeouts and a record seven no-hit games ... On this day in **1965 Jock Stein** was appointed manager of Celtic. He went on to become the club's most successful manager and in 1967 guided them to Britain's first victory in the European Cup. Between 1966 and 1974 Celtic won nine consecutive League titles, appeared in nine consecutive League Cup finals (winning five), and won five of the eight Scottish FA Cup finals they played in ... On this day in **1987 Adrian Sprott** scored in the seventieth minute for Hamilton in their shock Scottish FA Cup win over Glasgow Rangers. It was the first goal conceded by Rangers' keeper Chris Woods in 1196 minutes of play, a British record. He had kept clean sheets in 12 consecutive games between 29 November 1986 and 24 January 1987.

# FEBRUARY

**1** This day is dominated by football and footballers ... **Sir Stanley Matthews,** the first footballer to be knighted, was born on this day in **1915.** He started his career with Stoke City and then moved to Blackpool where, in 1953, he won the FA Cup winners' medal that seemed to be eluding him; he was 38 at the time. Matthews returned to Stoke in 1961 and on 6 February 1965, at the age of 50 years and six days, he played his last game, against Fulham. He is the oldest man to appear in the first division of the Football League. He made 701 League appearances and played for England 54 times ... In **1930 Joe Bambrick** created a British record when he scored six goals for Northern Ireland in their 7–0 win over Wales at Belfast ... In **1958** the **'Busby Babes'** played their last game on British soil, winning 5–4 at Highbury in a thrilling game. A crowd of over 63,000 saw Tommy Taylor (2), Bobby Charlton, Duncan Edwards and Dennis Viollet score for United. Five days later the heart of the team was ripped out in the Munich Air Disaster (*see 6 February*) ... In **1979 Brian Clough,** the Nottingham Forest manager, paid Birmingham City £1 million for Trevor Francis, the first British player to be the subject of a seven-figure transfer fee.

**2** The last bare-knuckle boxing champion, **John L. Sullivan,** died in **1918.** He lost to James J. Corbett in the first officially recognized world heavyweight title bout under Queensberry Rules in 1892, although some boxing historians believe Sullivan's win over Dominick McCaffrey at Cincinnati in 1885 was the first such contest. Sullivan continued boxing until 1905 when he fought a three-round exhibition with Jack McCormick at Grand

Rapids, Michigan. He was 46 years of age at the time (*see 7 September*).

**3**

In **1990** American jockey **Willie Shoemaker** had his 40,351st and last ride, on Patchy Groundfog at Santa Anita in the appropriately named 'The Legend's Last Ride Handicap' ... **Runcorn Highfield** drew 12–12 with Carlisle on 3 February **1991** to end the worst losing streak in rugby league history. The team had lost their previous 55 league games, going back to 29 January 1989. Their first win came 20 games later, in March 1991 (*see 3 March*).

**4**

American golfer **Byron Nelson** was born in **1912.** His 52 wins on the US tour put him in fifth place in the all-time table of total numbers of victories. Twenty-six of his wins came in just two seasons, 1944–45, with 18 of them achieved in the latter year, a record. Between March and August 1945 he won all 11 events he entered, including the PGA Championship. Nelson won the Masters twice, the PGA Championship twice, and in 1939 won the US Open after a three-way play-off ... This day seems to have been a lucky one for **Malcolm Campbell**. In **1927** he set a new world land speed record of 174.88 mph (281 km/hr) in his famous *Bluebird* at Pendine Sands, Wales. Exactly twelve months later, in **1928,** he increased it to 206·96 mph (333 km/hr) at Daytona Beach, Florida ... At Wellington in **1991** a record-breaking Test partnership between New Zealand batsmen **Martin Crowe and Andrew Jones** ended at 467 when Crowe was dismissed with the last ball of the day for 299. The pair had been at the crease for two days, helping their side to a total of 671 runs for 4 wickets against Sri Lanka. The Sri Lankans' first innings total of 497–9 declared was also a record, their highest in Test cricket. The match ended in a draw ... Also on this day in **1991** the **RFU** rejected a plea by Wimbledon FC to play their home matches at Twickenham.

**5**

At Melbourne in **1923, Victoria** became the first side in first-class cricket to amass a four-figure total of runs. Bill Ponsford scored 429 of Victoria's 1059 runs, against Tasmania, to establish an individual world record (*see 28 December*) ... Baseball player **Henry Louis ('Hank') Aaron** was born in **1934.** He holds the record for the most home runs in major league baseball, in 1974 he beat 'Babe' Ruth's 40-year record of 714 and ended his career with a total of 755 ... In **1974** only 450 turned up at Spotland (*see 6 December*) to watch the game between fourth division clubs **Rochdale and Cambridge,** the lowest attendance recorded at a Football League match, played under normal conditions.

**6**

The most famous baseball player of all-time, **'Babe' Ruth,** was born in **1895,** as George Herman Ruth. Originally a pitcher, he went on to become the greatest batter in the history of the game, and helped establish the New York Yankees as one of the top teams in the 1930s. He scored 2174 runs and 714 home runs during his career ... Former England soccer captain **Billy Wright** was born in **1924.** The first man to win 100 international caps, he captained England a record 90 times (since equalled by Bobby Moore) ... Former England fast bowler **Fred Trueman** was born in **1931.** The first man to take 300 Test wickets, he played for England 67 times ... This day in **1958** was one of the blackest in British soccer history, when eight members of the famous **Manchester United** team moulded by Matt Busby perished in an air crash at Munich Airport. Busby's 'Babes' were on their way home after beating Red Star Belgrade to reach the semi-final of the European Cup when their BEA Elizabethan crashed on take-off after refuelling at Munich ... In **1961** footballer **Danny Blanchflower** became the first person to refuse to appear on *This Is Your Life* ... **Stanley Matthews** played his last Football League game in **1965,** at the age of 50 years and six days (*see 1 February*).

**7**

**Gerald Davies,** one of the finest all-round rugby players, was born in **1945**. His acceleration and sidesteps were as fine as any seen in the game and were a major factor in the success of the Welsh international side in the 1970s. He played for Wales 46 times and scored a record 20 tries. He also toured with the Lions in 1968 and 1971 ... Top German swimmer **Kristin Otto** was born in **1965.** At Seoul in 1988 she set a women's Olympic record by winning six gold medals, just one short of Mark Spitz's all-time record haul at one Games (*see 10 February*). She took gold in the 100 metres freestyle, butterfly and backstroke, 50 metres freestyle, and in the 4 × 100 metres freestyle and medley relays. Previously she had won seven gold medals at the world championships in 1982 and 1986 ... **Joan Bazely** made history at Croydon, Surrey, in **1976** by becoming the first woman to referee a soccer match between two male teams ... And on the very same day at Stratford in **1976,** jockey **Diane Thorne** also went into the record book, as the first woman to ride a winner under National Hunt rules; her mount was Ben Ruler ... Ill-health forced **Bob Paisley** to quit the Liverpool board of directors in **1992,** ending a relationship with the club that had lasted since he joined them as a player, from Bishop Auckland, in 1939. He had to wait until after the war before making his debut. A successful playing career was followed by a stint on the coaching staff at Liverpool and, in 1974, the call to replace Bill Shankly as manager. Paisley went on to become the most successful manager in English soccer (*see 23 January*).

**8** Top Italian showjumper **Raimondo d'Inzeo** was born in **1925.** World champion in 1956 and 1960, he also won the Olympic title on Posillipo in 1960 ... The most infamous kidnapping in sport took place on this day in **1983** when the 1981 record breaking 10-length Derby winner **Shergar** was stolen from a stable in Ireland. A £2 million ransom was demanded but not paid. The horse, owned by the Aga Khan, was never seen again.

**9** Back in **1540** the **first recorded horserace meeting** in England took place at Chester's Roodee Fields ... The former England cricketer **Jim Laker** was born on this day in **1922.** He spent most of his career with the great Surrey team of the 1950s. In 46 Test appearances for England, Laker took 193 wickets. His most remarkable year was 1956: at Old Trafford he took 19 Australian wickets for 90 runs; and at the Oval, for Surrey, he took another 10 wickets in an innings, also against the Australians. Laker died in 1986 (*see 23 April and 31 July*) ... Gallacher and Lyle, the Ryder Cup golfers not the pop group, both enjoy birthdays today. **Bernard Gallacher,** who was appointed Ryder Cup captain in 1989 in succession to Tony Jacklin, was born in **1949. Sandy Lyle,** the first British Open winner for 16 years in 1985, was born in **1958.** Lyle went on to become the first British winner of the US Masters in 1988.

## 10

Tennis player **Bill Tilden** was born in **1893.** Tilden was the first US winner of the Wimbledon singles title in 1920. He also won a record-equalling seven US titles . . . **Mark Spitz,** the swimmer who won a record seven gold medals at the 1972 Munich Olympics, was born in **1950.** He won nine Olympic golds during his career, and set 26 world records . . . Australian golfer **Greg Norman** was born in **1958.** Known as the 'Great White Shark' Norman won the 1986 British Open aided by a round of 63. He regained the title in 1993 . . . The **first Oxford–Cambridge University rugby match,** at The Parks, ended in a win for the dark blues . . . The quarter-final of the southern section of the **1987** Freight Rover Trophy, between **Aldershot and Fulham,** was decided by a penalty shoot-out of epic proportions. A score line of 1–1 at the end of extra time was transformed into a 11–10 win for Aldershot, after a British record 28 penalties . . . In **1992,** and exactly two years to the day after losing his world title to Buster Douglas, **Mike Tyson** was found guilty of rape (*see 26 March*).

## 11

**John Surtees,** the only man to win world titles on two and four wheels, was born in **1934.** After winning four 500cc and three 350cc motor cycling world titles between 1956 and 1960, Surtees switched to the four-wheel branch of motor sport. In 1964, driving a Ferrari, he captured the world title. Surtees won six races in 111 starts, including the first victory for Honda in formula one, the 1967 Italian Grand Prix. He formed his own team later, but failed to register a victory in 118 starts ... At Innsbruck in **1976 John Curry** became the first British man to win the Olympic figure-skating title and the first Briton to win a gold medal in skating since Jeanette Altwegg in 1952 ... The biggest shock in world Heavyweight boxing history occurred in Tokyo in **1990** when the seemingly invincible **Mike Tyson** was knocked out in the 10th round by James 'Buster' Douglas. The fight was not without controversy. Douglas was floored in the eighth round and because of a mistake with the count was allowed to stay on the canvas for about 12 seconds. Tyson's camp was furious, reckoning he should have been counted out; Douglas's supporters retorted that he had been guided by the referee's count and could have got to his feet whenever he wanted. The arguments went on for days, but the decision was not reversed ... On the same day that Mike Tyson lost his world title in **1990, Leeds** established a rugby league first division record by beating Barrow 90–0.

**12**

In **1861** football teams from the neighbouring **Sheffield and Hallam** clubs met at Sheffield to play the first inter-club game of soccer ... British athlete **Steve Backley** was born in **1969.** He emerged as the finest male javelin thrower produced by Britain, first breaking the world record in July 1990 and in 1992 becoming the first man to throw 300 feet (91 m) with the modified javelin now used in competition. Despite his world record achievements, Backley disappointed in the 1990 Olympics, winning only a bronze medal.

**13**

In **1989** the Pakistan cricketer **Shoaib Mohammad** took a staggering 12 hours to score 163 runs against New Zealand at Wellington. It took him a record 11.5 hours to reach 150 ... The popular BBC television commentator **Ron Pickering** died in **1991** at the age of 60. A renowned coach, he guided Lynn Davies to the 1964 Olympic long jump gold medal ... **Liverpool** signed the biggest shirt sponsorship deal in Football League history on this day in **1992** when they signed a four-year contract worth £4 million with brewers Carlsberg.

**14**

**England dismissed South Africa** for 30 runs at Port Elizabeth in **1896;** George Lohmann took eight wickets for seven runs. The innings stood as the lowest in a Test match until 1955 (*see 28 March*) ... American jockey **Johnny Longden** was born at Wakefield, Yorkshire, in **1907.** He rode Count Fleet to victory in the US Triple Crown—that is the Kentucky Derby, the Belmont Stakes and the Preakness Stakes—in 1943. During 40 years as a jockey he rode 6032 winners, and was the first man to pass the 6000 mark ... In **1925,** in a Rugby League Northern Cup (now the Challenge Cup) match, **Wigan beat Cumberland amateurs Flimby and Fothergill** 116–0. Full back Jim Sullivan kicked a British record 22 goals ... Former England soccer star **Kevin Keegan** was born in **1951.** He started his career with Scunthorpe, then moved to Liverpool where he became a favourite with the Kop—until he left for Hamburg in 1977! He returned to Britain to play for first Southampton and then Newcastle. In 1992 he came out of retirement in Spain to manage Newcastle, guiding them to the Premier League in the 1992–93 season ... British skaters **Torvill and Dean** captured their Olympic title at Sarajevo in **1984** in impeccable style. Their performance—to Ravel's *Bolero*—wowed crowd and judges, and yielded them no fewer than 19 maximums ... In **1989 Peter Scudamore** became the third jockey, after Stan Mellor and John Francome, to ride 1000 National Hunt winners.

## 15

One of the best-known personalities in motor racing, **Graham Hill,** was born on this day in **1929.** World champion with BRM in 1962, he lifted the title a second time, in 1968, with Lotus. He won the Monaco Grand Prix five times. He also had success in endurance races, in 1966 winning the Indianapolis 500, and in 1972 the Le Mans 24-hour race. He was killed in a plane crash in 1975 (*see 29 November*) ... In the fifth Test at Melbourne in **1932 Australia beat South Africa** by an innings and 72 runs in the lowest scoring Test match of all time. In the first innings South Africa were dismissed for 36 in less than an hour and a half; Australia did somewhat better with a modest 153. In their second innings South Africa were again skittled out in less than 90 minutes, this time for 45 runs. The match, which was completed in two days, yielded a mere 234 runs from 109 overs ... In **1960** Australian wicketkeeper **Wally Grout** made a name for himself while playing for Queensland at Brisbane by dismissing eight batsmen in one innings, a world record in first-class cricket ... On the same day 20 years later, in **1980,** another wicketkeeper, **Bob Taylor** of England, equalled the Test world record by dismissing seven Indian batsmen (all caught) at Bombay.

**16** **England beat Australia** by six wickets to win the fourth Test match at Brisbane in **1933** and thus regain the Ashes in the infamous 'Bodyline' series (*see 17 January*) ... The brilliant but temperamental tennis star **John McEnroe** was born in **1959.** He won the singles at Wimbledon in 1981, 1983 and 1984 and also captured the doubles title five times ... At Leeds in **1991, Great Britain beat France 60–4** to register their biggest win in a rugby league international ... **Martina Navratilova** beat Jana Novotna in the Chicago Virginia Slims in **1992** to become the most successful Tennis player of all-time; it was the 158th title of her career.

**17** American basketball player **Michael Jordan** was born in **1963.** The leading scorer among current NBA players, he has accumulated more than 19,000 points for the Chicago Bulls, with an average of more than 32 points per game. Jordan was the world's highest paid sportsman in 1991–92 ... **Jean-Claude Killy** of France, one of the greatest Alpine skiers of all time, won his third gold medal at the **1968** Winter Olympics at Grenoble. Victorious in the downhill, the giant slalom and finally, the slalom, he equalled Toni Sailer's record of winning three gold medals at one Games (*see 17 November*).

**18** During England's record 13–0 win over Ireland on this day in **1882, Oliver Vaughton** (5 goals) and **Arthur Brown** (4) became the first England players to score hat-tricks in a full soccer international ... The man who built the Ferrari car empire, **Enzo Ferrari,** was born in **1898.** A racing driver with Alfa Romeo in the 1920s, he took over the team when Alfa quit racing at the end of 1929 and started manufacturing cars under the Scuderia Ferrari banner. Since the launch of the world motor-racing championship in 1950, Ferrari has been the most successful manufacturer and the only one to register 100 grand prix wins. Enzo Ferrari died in 1988 ... The former football player and England manager **Bobby Robson** was born in **1933.** He played 584 League games for West Bromwich and Fulham before becoming a manager and eventually making his name at Ipswich Town, leading them to a famous FA Cup win in 1978. Appointed manager of England in 1982, he guided the team to the semi-finals of the 1990 World Cup before returning to league soccer in Holland ... The first officially recognized world heavy-weight boxing champion under Queensberry Rules, **'Gentle-man' Jim Corbett**, died on this day in **1933.** He was 66 ... Footballer **Roberto Baggio** was born in **1967.** In 1990 he became the world's costliest footballer when he moved from Fiorentina to Juventus for £7.7 million.

## 19

The **first speedway meeting on a cinder track** took place in **1928** at High Beech, Essex ... In **1975** Her Majesty the Queen knighted cricketer **Gary Sobers** during a state visit to Barbados. Sobers was the fifth cricketer to be so honoured ... **Alan Shearer** scored on his England debut against France at Wembley in **1992.** England won 2–0 as France suffered their first defeat in 20 games. Shearer made his name with South-ampton before moving to Blackburn for a record fee of £3·6 million later in the year (*see 27 July*).

**20** Another prolific goalscorer, **Jimmy Greaves,** was born in **1940.** He started his career with Chelsea as a 17-year-old. He scored on his debut for the club and subsequently in every major competition he played in. His tally of 44 goals for England is bettered only by Gary Lineker (48) and Bobby Charlton (49). He was a member of the 1966 England World Cup squad, but was not picked to play in the final. In addition to Chelsea he also played for Spurs and West Ham and had a spell in Italy with AC Milan. Later he overcame alcoholism to enjoy a successful career in journalism and broadcasting. He popularized the phrase 'Funny 'ole game' ... The Shell Trophy cricket match between **Wellington and Canterbury** at Christchurch in **1990** was bizarre to say the least. In a deliberate attempt to give away runs in order to force a result, Wellington bowler Bert Vance delivered 17 no-balls in the penultimate over. The umpire inadvertently counted the number of legitimate balls, only five of which were delivered. The 22-ball over resulted in 77 runs being scored, 69 of them from the bat of wicket-keeper Lee Germon. A further 17 runs were scored off the last over. Canterbury faced the last ball needing just one run for victory, but the batsman offered no stroke and the match was drawn. Wellington still went on to win the Shell Trophy.

**21** One of the best-known members of the famous 'Busby Babes', **Duncan Edwards,** died in **1958** at the age of 21. The brightest prospect in English soccer, Edwards had made his international debut at the age of 18. He was a member of the great Manchester United team decimated in the Munich Air Disaster. Edwards clung to life for two weeks after the crash before eventually succumbing ... Playing in the Indian national snooker championship in **1988, Geet Sethi** became the first amateur to register an official maximum 147 break in a tournament.

## 22

Austrian motor-racing driver **Niki Lauda** was born in **1949.** He won his first world title with Ferrari in 1975. Only an horrific accident in the German Grand Prix at the Nürburgring in August 1976, which left him with severe facial burns and lung damage, prevented a second successive title. He regained his world crown from James Hunt a year later. He came out of retirement to win his third title with McLaren in 1984. He retired for good in 1985 to concentrate on running his successful airline company, Lauda Air ... in **1956 Portsmouth and Newcastle United** contested the first Football League game played under floodlights. Newcastle won 2–0 ... **Brian Bevan,** the top try-scorer in rugby league history, played his final match on this day in **1964.** He spent 17 years with Warrington before moving to Blackpool Borough where he remained until his retirement. He scored 796 tries between 1946 and 1964. He died in 1991 (*see 3 June*) ... Leading American tennis player **Michael Chang** was born in **1972** ... The second round Scottish FA Cup tie between **Inverness Thistle and Falkirk** was played in **1979** – at last! It had been postponed a (British) record 29 times because of bad weather ... In **1991** Liverpool manager **Kenny Dalglish** made the shock announcement of his retirement shortly after Liverpool's memorable 4–4 draw with Everton in the FA Cup. Dalglish returned to football a few months later to take charge of Blackburn Rovers.

**23**

In **1874 Major Walter Clopton Wingfield** patented his game of 'Sphairistike', which later became known as lawn tennis. He had demonstrated the new game to friends on the lawn of a house at Nantclwyd, Wales, during a Christmas party two months earlier ... Pakistan wicketkeeper **Wasim Bari** caught seven New Zealand batsmen during the Auckland Test match in **1979,** a Test record which England's Bob Taylor equalled a year later (*see 15 February*).

**24**

A mixed bag of sporting birthdays today ... **Brian Close,** the youngest man to play Test cricket for England, was born in **1931.** He spent most of his career with Yorkshire but enjoyed a successful end to his career at Somerset. He was 18 years and 149 days old when he made his Test debut in 1949. He was still playing for England in 1976, past his 45th birthday ... Scottish international footballer **Dennis Law** was born in **1940.** He scored a record 30 goals for his country in 55 appearances. At club level he played for Huddersfield Town and Manchester City before moving to Italy. On his return he joined City's local rivals, Manchester United. Ironically, he ended his career at City, and with his last kick in first-class football, in 1974, effectively relegated Manchester United to the second division. Dennis is now a much sought after match summarizer on radio and television ... **Alain Prost,** the first Frenchman to win the world motor-racing title, was born in **1955.** He won the world title with McLaren in 1985, retained it the following year and in 1989 won it a third time, also in a McLaren. He failed to find a drive in 1992 and spent the season out of the sport. He returned in 1993 as No 1 driver for Williams. In 1993 he became the first man to win 50 formula one races ... The European Soccer Championship qualifier between **Scotland and England** at Hampden Park in **1968** drew a crowd of 134,461, an attendance record for the championship ... In **1993** the former England soccer captain **Bobby Moore** died of cancer at the age of 51 (*see 12 April*).

**25**

**Paul Elvström,** the most successful yachtsman in Olympic history, was born in **1928.** He was the first man to win gold medals at four successive Olympics, 1948–60 ... Australian athlete **Herb Elliott** was born in **1938.** Elliott won the Commonwealth Games 880 yards and mile titles in 1958 and that same year, in Dublin, he reduced the world mile record to 3 min 54·5 sec. He won the Olympic 1500 metres title in 1960 ... Jamaican athlete **Don Quarrie** was born in **1951.** The Olympic 200 metres champion, he also won five individual Commonwealth Games sprint gold medals ... Ulster motor cyclist **Joey Dunlop** was born in **1952.** He equalled Mike Hailwood's career record of 14 TT wins in 1992. In both 1985 and 1988 he won three TTs in one week ... At Miami Beach, Florida, in **1964,** the 8–1 underdog **Cassius Clay** became heavyweight champion of the world when he stopped the defending champion Sonny Liston, who failed to come out for the seventh round ... In **1989 Frank Bruno** lost to Mike Tyson in his second attempt to win the world heavyweight title ... **Pakistan** were dismissed for 43 runs by the West Indies at Cape Town in **1993,** the lowest score in a completed innings in a one-day international.

**26** The **Grand National** was run at Aintree for the first time in 1839. The race, which was then known as the Grand Liverpool Steeplechase, was won by Lottery, ridden by Jem Mason. There had been three previous runnings of the race at nearby Maghull. In 1847 the race was renamed the Grand National Steeplechase ... In **1918** more than 600 people were killed when a stand collapsed at the **Hong Kong Jockey Club** ... Arsenal goalkeeper **Pat Jennings** fittingly kept his slate clean in a goalless draw at West Bromwich in **1983** on the occasion of his 1000th appearance in first-class football, a British record ... In **1993** Australian captain **Allan Border** became the most prolific scorer in Test cricket when he surpassed Sunil Gavaskar's record of 10,122 runs against New Zealand at Christchurch.

**27** South African Test cricketer **Graeme Pollock** was born in 1944. This stylish batsmen was probably the best left-hander in the world, but politics restricted his Test appearances, depriving cricketing fans of a full appreciation of his talent. He played in just 23 Test matches, scoring 2256 runs at an average of 60.97 ... In **1959 Boston Celtics scored 173 points against Minneapolis.** It was a new National Basketball Association (NBA) record points total and to this day remains the highest score in any game not needing extra time ... In **1990 Cambridge United** became the first fourth division side for 14 years to reach the sixth round of the FA Cup after beating Bristol City ... In **1991, Tony Adams** played his first game for Arsenal after his release from prison. He led the team to a 1–0 win over Shrewsbury Town in an FA Cup tie.

## 28

In 1914 **Huddersfield** established a rugby league record by beating Swinton Park Rangers 119–2 in the first round of the Northern Union Cup (now the Challenge Cup). They scored 27 tries and kicked 19 goals. Major Holland scored 39 points ... BBC golf commentator **Peter Alliss** was born in 1931. The son of Ryder Cup golfer Percy Alliss, Peter followed in his father's footsteps and also represented Britain in the competition (until 1979 the Ryder Cup was contested between Britain and the US, rather than Europe and the US). A respected golf expert and teacher, German-born Alliss won the Open titles of Portugal, France and Spain (twice), as well as the British PGA title on two occasions ... **Barry McGuigan** was born in 1951. The Ulsterman, known as 'The Clones Cyclone', turned professional in 1981. In 1985 he beat Eusebio Pedroza to win the WBA featherweight title and end Pedroza's seven-year reign as champion. After two successful defences, McGuigan lost the title to Steve Cruz in the Las Vegas heat ... **Colin Milburn,** the popular Northants and England cricketer, died suddenly at the age of 48 in 1990 ... in 1993 **Tom Kite** became the first golfer to win $8 million in a career on the US PGA Tour.

## 29

At Worcester in 1984 **John Francome** became the second National Hunt jockey, after Stan Mellor, to ride 1000 winners ... At St Andrews in 1992 the game between **Birmingham City and Stoke City** was halted by the worst scenes of hooliganism witnessed in recent years at a British football match. Referee Roger Wiseman was hit by a spectator during the 20-minute stoppage and subsequently withdrew from the list of Football League referees, citing 'mental stress' as the reason for his decision.

# MARCH

**1**

**In 1936** Golden Miller, ridden by Evan Williams, won his fifth consecutive Cheltenham Gold Cup ... On St David's Day in **1940,** Welsh showjumper **David Broome** was born. Broome won the world championship in 1970, on Beethoven, the only male British rider to have done so. His sister Liz, later Liz Edgar, was also a top class showjumper ... The reigning world heavyweight boxing champion **Joe Louis,** known as 'The Brown Bomber', announced his retirement in **1949,** nine months after making his 25th, and last, successful defence of the title. He came out of retirement the following year to challenge the new champion, Ezzard Charles. This defeat and an eighth-round knockout by Rocky Marciano in 1951 persuaded Louis to quit permanently (*see 25 June*) ... In **1958 Gary Sobers** completed the highest ever innings in Test cricket when he made an unbeaten 365 for West Indies against Pakistan at Kingston, Jamaica. Sobers beat Len Hutton's old record by one run ... New York Yankees baseball star **Mickey Mantle** retired on this day in **1969**. He took his number, seven, with him, an honour previously paid only to Babe Ruth, Lou Gehrig and Joe DiMaggio. One of baseball's all-time greats, Mantle broke Babe Ruth's record of 16 World Series home runs and established a new one of his own—his 18 runs remains a record. Mantle hit a grand total of 536 home runs in his 18-year career ... At Murrayfield in **1975** a world record crowd of 104,000 watched the rugby international between **Scotland and Wales** ... Former prolific goalscorer **Dixie Dean** died in **1980** shortly after watching his former team Everton lose 2–1 at home to Liverpool in the Merseyside 'derby'.

**2**  Two well-known sports personalities were born on this day in **1949.** The first, **J.P.R. Williams,** is one of Welsh rugby's most revered players, and its most-capped. He played for Wales 55 times and also made eight appearances for the British Lions ... Yachtswoman **Naomi James** sailed round the world single-handed in 1977–78, and during her voyage became the first woman to sail solo round Cape Horn ... Another Welshman has a birthday today: **Ian Woosnam,** who was born in **1958.** He was the first British winner of the World Match-Play title, in 1987. In that same year he helped Wales to win the World Cup and in the process also carried off the individual title. He won the US Masters in 1991 ... At Hershey, Pennsylvania, in **1962, Wilt Chamberlain** of the Philadelphia Warriors became the first and only man to score 100 points in a National Basketball Association (NBA) game. Philadelphia beat the New York Knicks 169–147 in front of a crowd of 4124.

**3**  On this day in **1928 Ronnie Dix** made history as the youngest person to score a goal in the Football League. He was only 15 years and 180 days old when he netted for Bristol Rovers in their 3–0 win over Norwich in a third division (south) game ... In **1936** Australia's **Victor Richardson** set a record during a Test match against South Africa at Durban by holding five catches, the most by an outfielder in an innings of Test cricket ... Rugby international **Ollie Campbell** was born in **1954.** One of the most prolific scorers in Irish rugby, he accumulated a then record 246 points between 1976 and 1984. The total of 52 points he scored in the 1983 International Championship, including 21 against England, was also a record ... Top British javelin thrower **Fatima Whitbread** was born in **1961.** She won the world title in 1987 and the following year took the silver medal at the Seoul Olympics to add to her bronze from Los Angeles in 1984 . . . In **1991 Runcorn Highfield's** dismal record of 75 matches without a win ended when they beat Dewsbury. Their run, the worst in rugby league history, went back 28 months during which time they had five coaches!

**4**

**George West** scored a record 11 tries in a rugby league match while playing for Hull Kingston Rovers against Brookland Rovers in the Northern Cup (now the Challenge Cup) in **1905** . . . British motor-racing champion **Jim Clark** was born in Fife in Scotland in **1936.** World champion in 1963 and 1965, he was unquestionably one of the all-time greats of motor racing. He died tragically young while racing at Hockenheim, Germany, in 1968 (*see 7 April*) . . . Another Scot, the former Celtic and Liverpool footballer, **Kenny Dalglish,** was born in **1951.** The only man to play for Scotland 100 times, he won every honour at club level as a player before going on to manage top clubs Liverpool and Blackburn . . . What snooker player **Willie Thorne,** born in **1954,** lacks in tournament wins—the 1985 Mercantile Credit Classic is his only ranking tournament success—he makes up for in personality as one of the game's most popular players . . . In **1967** third division **Queen's Park Rangers brought off a shock 3–2 win over West Bromwich Albion** in the first Football League Cup final to be played at Wembley . . . In **1976 John Curry** added to his Olympic gold medal by winning the men's title at the world figure-skating championships.

**5** The most successful goal-kicker in modern rugby league, **David Watkins,** was born in **1942.** A former Welsh rugby union international, he played for his country 21 times and for the Lions on six occasions. A fly-half, he switched to the professional code and soon adapted to the 13-a-side game. His tally of 221 goals for Salford in the 1972–73 season is a rugby league record ... **Ernie Terrell,** brother of Jean Terrell, a former member of the Supremes vocal group, beat Eddie Machen to win the WBA heavyweight title in **1965.** Cassius Clay had captured the title by beating Sonny Liston a year earlier but, because he refused to put a re-match clause into the contract, the WBA withdrew recognition of him as champion. When Clay and Terrell eventually met, the judges were unanimous in declaring Clay (then Muhammad Ali) the winner at the end of the 15-round contest.

**6** **Ernest Michaux** of France won the first international cycle race, at the Crystal Palace, in **1869** ... **Dick Fosbury,** the man who added a new word to the vocabulary of track and field athletics, was born in **1947.** He revolutionized the high jump at the 1968 Olympics by leaping backwards over the bar to take the gold medal. Once it was decided this was legal, most high jumpers copied his style, which became known as the 'Fosbury Flop' ... **Accrington Stanley** were forced to withdraw their membership from the Football League on this day in **1962.** They were only the second team, after Wigan Borough in 1931–32, to pull out of the League after the start of the season; a similar fate would befall Aldershot in 1991–92. Accrington had played 33 of their 46 fixtures at the time of their demise. Their

last match was on 4 March when they lost 4–0 at Crewe ...
American-born motor-racing driver **Mario Andretti** enjoyed
the first grand prix win of his career in **1971** when he won the
South African Grand Prix at Kyalami in a Ferrari. It was the
first of 12 wins for Andretti, who won the world title in 1978
... In **1976, Wilfred (then Wilfredo) Benitez** of Puerto Rico
became the youngest-ever world boxing champion at the age of
17 years and 176 days when he beat Antonio Cervantes to win
the WBA junior-welterweight title at San Juan.

**7**

Former West Indian cricket captain **Viv Richards** was born in
**1952.** He registered his best Test score, of 291, at the Oval in
1976. His total of 1710 runs that year represents the highest
score by a batsman in one calendar year. In 1984 he scored a
One-Day International record 189 not out against England at
Manchester. Two years later he scored a Test century, also
against England, off only 56 balls; the least number a batsman
has received to score 100 runs. In 121 matches for the West
Indies he scored a grand total of 8540 runs. Richards also played
County cricket for Somerset and Glamorgan ... Tennis player
**Ivan Lendl** was born in **1960.** The winner of eight Grand Slam
singles titles, Lendl came close to the Wimbledon title in 1986
and 1987, but on both occasions he was beaten in the final, first
by Boris Becker and in the following year by Pat Cash. His
career earnings of more than $19 million is a record in men's
tennis ... The great Australian racing driver **Jack Brabham**
enjoyed his 14th and last grand prix win in **1970,** at South
Africa's Kyalami circuit. Brabham's career was long by motor-
racing standards, lasting more than 15 years. He won the world

title three times, in 1959, 1960 and 1966. He is the only world motor-racing champion to win the championship (in 1966) in a car of his own design, the Brabham ... In **1991 Lennox Lewis** captured the British and European heavyweight titles by stopping defending champion Gary Mason in the seventh round of their bout at Wembley.

**8** British swimmer **David Wilkie** was born in **1955.** At the Montreal Olympics in 1976 he became the first British male swimmer to strike gold since 1908. He beat America's John Hencken by nearly two seconds to take the 200 metres breaststroke title in a world record time. Four days earlier the positions were reversed in the 100 metres final when Hencken won in a world-record time with Wilkie in the silver medal position ... In **1971 Muhammad Ali** failed to regain the heavyweight crown in his first world title fight since returning to the ring. He was beaten on points over 15 rounds by his arch rival Joe Frazier at Madison Square Garden, New York (*see 29 April*) ... In **1989,** Canada's **Cliff Thorburn** made history at the Hawth Centre, Crawley, by becoming the first snooker player to compile two officially ratified 147 breaks.

**9** American chess genius **Bobby Fischer** was born in **1943.** His world championship match with Boris Spassky at Reykjavik, Iceland, in 1972 turned the game into a multi-media spectacle. He lost his crown in 1975 when agreement could not be reached for a match against Anatoly Karpov, who took the title by default. In 1992 Fischer reappeared on the international chess scene and engaged in a hyped re-match against Spassky. Fischer won again ... The ex-England rugby captain **Bill Beaumont**

was born in **1952.** Lancashire-born Beaumont guided England to the Grand Slam in 1980, but retired shortly afterwards because of injury. His distinguished career included 34 international appearances and two British Lions tours. He soon added other strings to his bow, as a television summarizer and, of course, as one of the captains on the quiz game *A Question of Sport*. In the latter his, and opposing skipper Ian Botham's, desire to win remains insatiable . . . Also celebrating his birthday on this day is St Helens boxer **John Lyon,** born in **1962.** He is British amateur boxing's most successful fighter, with a record eight ABA (Amateur Boxing Association) titles to his credit (1981–89) . . . In **1991** Atlético Madrid goalkeeper **Abel Resino** set a new world record by going 1224 minutes without conceding a goal. His unbeaten run eventually ended at 1274 minutes on 17 March when he conceded a goal after 50 minutes of a 3–1 home win v Sporting Gijon.

**10**

At Baroda, India, in **1947** the fourth wicket partnership of **Gulzar Mahomed and Vijay Hazare** produced 577 runs against visiting Holkar, a world record in first-class cricket. Hazare celebrated his 32nd birthday the following day . . . One of the smallest men to win a world boxing title, **Jimmy Wilde,** died in **1969.** Born at Tylorstown, Rhondda, South Wales, in 1892, the aptly nicknamed 'Mighty Atom' (he rarely tipped the scales above 108 lb/49 kg) began his professional career at the age of 19. Wilde won 126 of his 140 pro fights, 77 of them by knockout. He won the world flyweight title in 1916 and made one officially recognized defence before losing it to Pancho Villa in 1923; that was Wilde's last fight . . . In **1992 David O'Leary** played his record 700th game for Arsenal (*see 17 March*).

## 11

**Malcolm Campbell,** who pioneered attempts to reach the limits of speed, was born in **1885.** He was the first man to build a machine specially for the purpose of setting new speed records on land and water. His creation, *Bluebird*, became synonymous with speed and the name was carried on in the craft developed by his son Donald (*see 4 January*). Malcolm died in December 1948 (*see 3 September*) ... In **1911** a crowd of 39,146 watched first-division **Bradford City beat second-division Burnley 1–0** in the FA Cup. The Valley Parade ground has not played host to such a large crowd since that day and so has the longest standing attendance record in the Football League ... American tennis player **Louise Brough** was born in **1928.** She won 35 Grand Slam titles, ten of them at Wimbledon, including the singles title four times between 1948 and 1955 ... Four times British Open golf champion **Bobby Locke** died in **1988** (*see 20 November*) ... **Jennifer Capriati** became the youngest finalist in a professional tennis tournament when, in **1990,** aged 13 years and 347 days, she reached the final of the Virginia Slims in Florida. She was beaten by Gabriela Sabatini of Argentina, who had previously held the record at 14 years and 11 months ... On the same day in **1990, Severiano Ballesteros** won his 60th European Tour event, the Balearic Open at Son Vida, Majorca.

## 12

At St George's Park, Port Elizabeth, in **1889 Test cricket** was played in South Africa for the first time. The host nation, led by O. R. Dunnell, entertained the England team skippered by Aubrey Smith in the first of two Tests. England won the first Test by eight wickets after dismissing South Africa for just 84 runs. What a debut! The England captain, Smith, later found fame as a Hollywood actor ... The **BBC televised its first athletics meeting** in 1938 when they covered the annual Oxford versus Cambridge match from the White City ... **Wendy Toms** made history as the first woman to officiate at a Football League game. She was selected as the fourth official for a third division game between Bournemouth and Reading in 1991 ... The former Cardiff City and Wales full-back **Alf Sherwood** died in 1991 at the age of 66. He played for Wales 41 times between 1947 and 1957.

## 13

The **Scottish Football Association** was formed on this day in 1873 when representatives of eight clubs met at the Dewar's Hotel, Glasgow ... The **1948 Lincolnshire Handicap** drew a field of 58 horses, the largest number of runners for a flat race in Britain ... Boxer **Joe Bugner** was born in 1950. Hungarian-born Bugner, who was brought to Britain as a youngster, captured the British, European and Commonwealth heavyweight titles with a controversial win over Henry Cooper in 1971. His potential was never fully realized and perhaps his finest achievement was in taking Muhammad Ali the distance in a world title fight in Kuala Lumpur in 1975 ... The former West Indian cricket captain **Sir Frank Worrell** died in 1967 at the age of 42. His international career for West Indies included 51 appearances and 3860 runs. In the 1945–46 season he and former schoolmate Clyde Walcott put on a then world record 574 (unbroken) for the fourth wicket for Barbados against Trinidad at Port-of-Spain. It was the second time Worrell had been involved in a partnership of 500 or more. Test matches between the West Indies and Australia are for the Frank Worrell Trophy ... While competing in the English Amateur Snooker Championship at Aldershot, Hampshire, in **1991, Ronnie O'Sullivan** (now a professional) became the youngest person to compile a maximum 147 break in competitive play. He was only 15 years and 98 days old at the time.

## 14

The 1984 women's Olympic javelin champion, **Tessa Sanderson,** was born in Jamaica in **1957.** After making two unsuccessful attempts at the Olympic title she eventually struck gold in Los Angeles in 1984, breaking the Olympic record with her first throw in the final. She was the first Briton, and first black athlete, to win an Olympic throwing title. She later became a television celebrity ... **Ken Barrington,** the former Surrey and England batsman, collapsed and died of a heart attack while touring with the England team in the West Indies in **1981.** In his playing days he was member of the Surrey team that won seven consecutive county championship titles in the 1950s. Barrington also played for England 82 times and scored 6806 runs at an average of 58·67.

## 15

The **Cincinnati Red Stockings,** the first professional baseball team, played their first match as professionals against Great Western in **1869 ... Test cricket** was inaugurated on this day in **1877** when James Lillywhite's touring England team met the Australians at the Melbourne cricket ground. Charles Bannerman (Australia) made history as the first man to score a century in Test cricket. Remarkably, when the Centenary Test was played 100 years later the result was exactly the same; an

Australian win by 45 runs ... Playing for Wales against England at Highbury in **1920, Billy Meredith** of Manchester United became the oldest person to play international soccer. He was aged 45 years and 229 days at the time. He played for both Manchester clubs during his 26-year career which also included 48 caps for Wales ... In **1947 Neil McBain** became the oldest person to play in the Football League when he kept goal for New Brighton in a third-division (north) match against Hartlepools United. Manager of New Brighton at the time, he was forced by a goalkeeper shortage to go in goal. Considering his age— 51 years 120 days—the score-line of 3–0 to Hartlepools seems respectable ... American jockey **Cash Asmussen** was born in **1962.** A winner of the Eclipse Award for top apprentice at the age of 17 in the 1979 season, with a total of 263 winners, he came to Europe in 1982. At Chepstow in 1993 he made history as the first American jockey to ride a winner for Her Majesty the Queen ... In **1990,** playing for New Zealand against Australia at Wellington, **Richard Hadlee** took five wickets in an innings for the 100th time in his career ... At San Sebastian, Spain, in **1991** the Ukrainian pole-vaulter **Sergey Bubka** became the first man to clear 20 feet (6.1 m) indoors.

**16** In **1872** the first FA Cup final was contested by the **Wanderers and the Royal Engineers**. A crowd of 2000 at the Kennington Oval saw the Wanderers' striker Betts score the only goal of the game ... In **1991 Simon Hodgkinson** kicked five goals for England against France in the rugby union International Championship, taking his tally to a championship record 60 for the season. The final score in the match was 21–19 to England.

**17**

Cornishman **Bob Fitzsimmons** beat 'Gentleman' Jim Corbett to win the world heavyweight title at Carson City, Nevada, in **1897.** He had already won the world middleweight title, in 1891. In 1903 he took the light-heavyweight title to become the first man to win three world titles. He is the only British-born fighter to win the heavyweight crown ... The finest amateur golfer of all-time, **Bobby Jones,** was born in **1902.** He never turned pro and was more than a match for his professional counterparts. He won the British Open three times and the US Open four times. His remarkable 'grand slam' of titles in 1930 will surely never be equalled (*see 27 September*). Jones was also responsible for designing and building the Augusta National golf course, and from there he came up with the idea of the US Masters. He died in 1971 ... In **1947 Rocky Marciano** won the first of his 49 professional fights when he beat Lee Epperson (*see 21 September*) ... In **1979 Wales beat England** at Cardiff to capture an unprecedented third successive rugby union Triple Crown ... The **1983** Cheltenham Gold Cup was dominated by horses from the stable of trainer **Michael Dickinson,** who saddled the first five past the post ... Four players received their marching orders (three from Rangers) during **Celtic's 2–0 win** in the 'Old Firm' clash at Parkhead in **1991** ... A week after playing his 700th game for Arsenal in **1992, David O'Leary** was sent off for the first time in his career, during a game for the reserve team.

**18**

Two famous Irishmen share their birthday today: snooker player **Alex Higgins** was born in **1949,** and top flat racing jockey **Pat Eddery** in **1952.** Higgins won two world titles, in 1972 and

1982. His brilliance was matched by a tendency to throw tantrums which increased as he slipped down the world rankings. Eddery, on the other hand, has stayed at the top since winning the first of nine jockey's titles in 1974. In 1990 he became the first man since Gordon Richards, in 1952, to ride 200 winners in a season ... Swedish skiier **Ingemar Stenmark** was born in **1956.** He won a record 86 World Cup races between 1974 and 1989 and was three times overall champion. He won slalom and giant slalom gold medals at the 1980 Winter Olympics ... **Oxford** set a record time for the Boat Race in **1984,** winning in 16 minutes and 45 seconds.

## 19

**Norman Yardley,** the former England and Yorkshire cricketer, was born in **1915.** He skippered his national side on 14 of the 20 occasions on which he played for them ... The **BBC televised its first rugby match** in **1938** when they covered the Calcutta Cup game between England and Scotland at Twickenham. Scotland won 21–16 and captured that season's championship ... England and Nottingham Forest striker **Nigel Clough** was born in **1966,** two days before his father's 31st birthday. The son of the Forest manager, Brian Clough, he has emulated his father by playing for England.

## 20

In **1898** the **first recorded international cross-country race** took place at Ville d'Avray near Paris. England beat the hosts over a nine-mile (14.5 km) course ... **Scotland beat England** at Twickenham for the first time in **1926;** the score was 17–9. They went on to share that season's championship with Ireland ... On the same day in **1937 England** gained revenge by winning 6–3 at Murrayfield. They went on to win their 11th Triple Crown . . . The top Russian goalkeeper **Lev Yaschin** died at the age of 60 in **1990.** He won 78 Soviet caps between 1952 and 1972 and is the first, and so far, only goalkeeper to win the European Footballer of the Year Award . . . This day in **1992** was a busy one for sport. **Aldershot FC,** which had been declared bankrupt in the High Court on 18 March, played their last Football League game, losing 2–0 away to Cardiff. The club became the first since Accrington Stanley in 1962 to withdraw from the League during the season. Their record of three wins and eight draws from 36 matches was deleted from the Football League records . . . On the same day that Aldershot were playing their last match in **1992,** the former Wales and Arsenal goalkeeper **Jack Kelsey** died at the age of 62. **John Oakes,** the former Charlton Athletic player, also died on this day. He was 86 . . . In the United States, also in **1992, Victor Kiam** agreed to sell his 51 per cent stake in the New England Patriots gridiron team for $50 million. **Tommy Hearns** lost his world light-heavyweight title on a split decision to Iran Barkley at Las Vegas.

**21** In **1874** a crowd of 3500 at the old Hampden Park ground saw **Queen's Park beat Clydesdale 2–0** in the first Scottish FA Cup final. Queen's Park went on to win the cup in its first three seasons . . . **Brian Clough,** who started the 1992–93 season as the longest-serving manager in the Football League, was born in **1935.** As a player, Clough was a brilliant goalscorer, netting 251 times in 274 League games, and was twice the Football League's top scorer in the 1950s. He played for Sunderland and

Middlesbrough, but his career was cut short by injury. He took up management, first with Hartlepool and then guiding Derby County to two first division titles. Spells at Brighton and Leeds United were less successful. He joined Nottingham Forest in 1975 and led them to promotion and the first division title in successive years. League Cup and European Cup glory also followed, but the FA Cup eluded 'Cloughie'. Sadly, he ended his 18-year term as Forest manager in 1993 with a drop from the Premier League to the First Division . . . Brazilian motor-racing champion **Ayrton Senna** was born in **1960.** He made his formula one debut with Toleman in 1984. Four years later he won his first world title, with McLaren. He regained it in 1990 and successfully defended it the following year with eight race wins. Senna was the second man, after Alain Prost, to accumulate 500 world championship points in a career. He has started more races from pole position than any other driver . . . The leading women's long-distance runner, **Ingrid Kristiansen**, was born in **1964.** Danish-born Kristiansen has set world best times at 5000 and 10,000 metres and in the marathon. She has won the world's leading marathons, including the London race four times, but Olympic gold has eluded her.

**22** An informal meeting of clubs interested in forming a **Football League** was held at Anderton's Hotel, Fleet Street, in **1888.** The first formal meeting took place on 17 April . . . The first rugby union international between **England and France** was played in Paris in **1906.** England won 35–8 . . . The **1929 Grand National** attracted a record field of 66 runners. The 100–1 winner was Gregalach, ridden by Bob Everett . . . Scotland's only world darts champion, **Jocky Wilson,** was born in **1950.** He has twice lifted the world crown, in 1982 when he beat John Lowe 5–3 and in 1989 when he defeated Eric Bristow 6–4 .

**23**

**Roger Bannister,** the first man to run one mile in under four minutes, was born in **1929.** In the same year as his record-breaking triumph, 1954, Bannister won the Commonwealth Games mile and the European 1500 metres titles. These were his only major international titles (*see 6 May*) . . . Cuban amateur boxer **Teofilio Stevenson** was born in **1952.** The only man to win the same Olympic title (heavyweight) three times, he resisted many offers to turn professional. Had there not been a boycott of athletes from Communist countries at the 1984 Los Angeles Olympics, Stevenson might well have added a fourth title. He also won three world amateur titles . . . **Mike Hailwood,** one of Britain's best-loved motor-cycle champions, died on this day in **1981.** He lost his life in a car accident near his home in Birmingham while going to buy fish and chips. His daughter Michelle also died in the crash. (*see 2 April*).

**24**

In **1877** the **Oxford–Cambridge Boat Race** ended in a dead-heat for the first and only time . . . In the **1922 Grand National** only three of the 32 starters finished. First over the finishing line was 100–9 shot Music Hall, ridden by Bilbie Rees . . . The former Scotland, Derby County, Nottingham Forest and Birmingham City footballer **Archie Gemmill** was born in **1947.** He played for Scotland 43 times. In the 1978 World Cup finals he scored one of the finest goals in the history of the tournament, weaving his way through the Dutch defence before unleashing a swerving shot into the corner of the net. His son Scot is now making a name for himself with Nottingham Forest ... Top American woman golfer **Pat Bradley** was born in **1951**. Twice LPGA Player of the Year, she has won all four of the ladies' major tournaments; in 1986 only the US Open eluded her. She is the all-time career money winner on the US Tour, with more than $4 million from 30–plus wins ... **Ian Woosnam** won his first golf tournament in the United States, beating Jim Hallet at the second extra hole in the **1991** USF and G Classic at New Orleans. Three weeks later he won his second—the Masters.

**25** **Wales** played their first international soccer match in **1876,** losing 4–0 to Scotland in Glasgow. Five years and eight matches later they had their first win, beating England 1–0 at Blackburn ... Two boys who would later become Britain's best middle-distance runners competed in the **1972** British Schools Cross-Country Championships, Intermediate division. **Steve Ovett** came home in second place while his great rival of the future, **Sebastian Coe,** finished down the list in tenth position ... In **1990** the **Welsh rugby union team** rounded off their worst-ever season in the International Championship with a 14–8 defeat by Ireland at Lansdowne Road. It was the first time they had lost all four games in a championship season ... **Aldershot FC** lost their fight for survival **(1992)** and folded with debts of £1·2 million.

## 26

The **first steeplechase** under National Hunt rules took place at Market Harborough, Leicestershire, in **1863.** The winning horse, Socks, was ridden by Mr Goodman ... In **1927 Ferdinando Minoaia and Giuseppe Morandi,** driving an OM, won the inaugural Mille Miglia at an average speed of 77·22 mph (124 km/hr). The race, from Brescia to Rome and back, was the most famous long-distance race of its time. A bad accident in the 1957 race forced changes which resulted in a smaller version of the event in subsequent years. The Mille Miglia was responsible for popularizing the Alfa Romeo, which won the race 11 times between 1928 and 1939 ... In **1959 Mushtaq Mohammad,** aged 15 years and 124 days, made his Test cricket debut for Pakistan against West Indies at Lahore. The youngest-ever man to play Test cricket, a record which still stands, he went on to become one of the world's top batsmen ... In **1992 Mike Tyson** received a six-year prison sentence for rape (*see 22 November*).

## 27

Leading woman downhill skier **Annemarie Moser-Proll** of Austria was born in **1953.** She won a record 62 World Cup races, a record seven downhill titles, and six overall titles. She also captured the Olympic downhill title in 1980 ... British Olympic swimmer **Duncan Goodhew** was born in **1957.** He came to prominence in the sport at a time when swimmers believed they could travel faster through the water by shaving their heads. Duncan had literally a head start over his rivals, having lost his hair permanently as a youngster because of a childhood accident. He beat the Soviet swimmer Arsen Miskarov to take the gold medal in the 100 metres breaststroke at the 1980 Moscow Olympics, but could only finish sixth in the 200 metres. Goodhew's mother was in the audience to watch her son win his gold medal, but his step-father supported the boycott of the Games, in protest at the Soviet invasion of Afghanistan, and refused to go . . . Great Britain international rugby league star **Ellery Hanley** was born in **1961.** He started his professional career with Bradford Northern and then big money tempted him to move across the Pennines to Wigan where he became the inspiration behind their success in the 1980s . . . The second division Football League game between Crystal Palace and Brighton in **1989** saw referee **Kelvin Morton** award a record five penalties. Only two of these were converted, one by each side; Palace won 2–1.

**28**

On this day in **1912** both boats capsized in the annual **University Boat Race** on the Thames. Oxford won the re-run race to register their fourth consecutive win. On the same date in **1925** the **Oxford** boat sank again . . . **New Zealand were dismissed by England** for just 26 runs at Auckland in **1955.** The innings, New Zealand's second, lasted a mere 27 overs. The figures for the England bowlers were: Statham 3 wickets for 9 runs; Tyson 2 wickets for 10 runs, Appleyard 4 wickets for 7 runs and Wardle 1 wicket for 0 runs. The innings stands as the lowest completed in Test cricket, surpassing the previous record of 30 which was twice achieved by South Africa, against England. England made 246 in the first innings and had a lead of just 46 runs when New Zealand went in for their second innings. Captain Len Hutton could hardly have imagined his side would win by an innings.

**29**

At Kennington Oval in **1890, William Townley** of Blackburn Rovers became the first man to score a hat-trick in an FA Cup final. Rovers trounced Sheffield Wednesday 6–1 in front of 20,000 fans. Only two other men, Jimmy Logan (Notts County v Bolton, 1894) and Stan Mortensen (Blackpool v Bolton, 1953) have emulated Townley's feat ... In **1927 Sir Henry Segrave** broke Malcolm Campbell's world land speed record when his car *Mystery* powered to a speed of 203·84 mph (327·97 km/hr) at Daytona Beach ... Two well-known motor-racing drivers enjoyed their first grand prix success on this day. In **1974** Argentine **Carlos Reutemann,** driving a Brabham, took the chequered flag in the South African Grand Prix at Kyalami ... In the **1980** US Grand Prix West at Long Beach, Brazil's **Nelson Piquet** had his first triumph, also in a Brabham. It was the first of 23 wins for the Brazilian, who captured the world title in 1981, 1983 and 1987 ... The **first London Marathon** was staged on this day in **1981.** Britain's Joyce Smith won the ladies' race while the men's title was shared by Dick Beardsley (USA) and Inge Simonsen (Norway) who crossed the line together. A total of 7000 runners took part in the inaugural race, which was the brainchild of the former British Olympic steeplechase champion Chris Brasher. These days, around 25,000 athletes take part ... In **1988 Lloyd Honeyghan** became the first British boxer since Ted 'Kid' Lewis in 1917 to regain a world title, beating Jorgé Vaca of Mexico with a knockout in the third round of their WBC welterweight bout at Wembley. Honeyghan had lost his title to Vaca five months earlier on a technical decision. When he took Donald Curry's Crown in 1986, Honeyghan achieved a rare distinction among British fighters by winning a world title *in* the United States. He stopped Curry in the sixth round of their bout at Atlantic City.

## 30

The **1895** Boat Race between **Oxford and Cambridge** Universities was the first regular British sporting event to be captured on film, by cameraman Bert Acres ... Everton and Wales goalkeeper **Neville Southall** made his 500th senior appearance in **1991**, against Aston Villa.

## 31

**Jack Johnson,** the first black man to win the world heavyweight boxing title, was born in **1872.** Because of the attitude towards blacks in the United States, he had to go to Australia to challenge Tommy Burns for the title in 1908. Johnson captured the title but was still forced to make most of his defences outside the United States. The boxing authorities put forward a succession of 'Great White Hopes' to take the title from him. All failed until a giant from Kansas, Jess Willard, beat him in 1915. Johnson maintained he was forced to throw the fight, and to this day many still believe this to have been the case (*see 5 April*) ... The world featherweight boxing contest between **Ike Weir and Frank Murphy** in **1889** ended in a draw after 80 rounds. The contest was stopped by the police. It is the longest world title fight under Queensberry Rules ... At Leicester in **1921** Jockey **Gordon Richards** rode his first winner, Gay Lord. It was the first of a record 4870 wins for Richards, Britain's most successful jockey ... The **England soccer team** suffered one of its most embarrassing defeats on this day in **1928** when Scotland came to Wembley and ran out 5–1 winners. Alec Jackson was the hero of the 'Wembley Wizards' with a hat-trick

... At Selhurst Park in **1961** a crowd of 37,774 watched the game between **Crystal Palace and Millwall.** It is an all-time record attendance for a fourth (now third) division game in the Football League ... In **1978** the 'Will he run? Won't he run?' saga of Red Rum was eventually resolved by trainer Ginger McCain who announced that 'Rummie' would not be taking part in his sixth Grand National due to injury. The great horse was retired. 'Rummie's' record of three wins in the race will be a hard one to equal ... **Jesse Owens,** the black American track and field star, whose success at the 1936 Olympics so infuriated Adolf Hitler, died on this day in **1980.**

# APRIL

# APRIL

**1** In 1933 **Walter Hammond** set a new world Test match record when he made 336 not out against New Zealand at Auckland. He surpassed Don Bradman's old record of 334, set three years earlier. Hammond's innings included a Test record ten sixes ... Welsh rugby international **J. J. Williams** was born in **1948.** He toured with the British Lions in 1974 and 1977 and won 30 Welsh caps ... The former England cricket captain **David Gower** was born in **1957.** He exceeded Geoff Boycott's career record of the most runs scored for England in 1992, but was surprisingly omitted from the winter tour to India later that year. His omission split the MCC membership ... The **Rangers versus Celtic** match from Ibrox in **1990** was the first British League game to be broadcast on satellite, by BSB, in Britain.

**2** Australian motor-racing driver **Jack Brabham** was born in **1926.** Brabham was world champion in 1959 and 1960, in both seasons with the Cooper-Climax team. He won his third title in 1966, becoming the first man to win the championship in his own car. Brabham continued to manufacture racing cars after his retirement in 1970 ... **Mike Hailwood**, one of Britain's most successful motor cyclists, was born in **1940.** He won a record 14 Isle of Man TT races, won 76 grand prix races and was world champion nine times, including four 500 cc titles for MV Agusta ... **Duncan Edwards** made his first appearance for England in a game against Scotland at Wembley Stadium in **1955;** England won 7–2. Aged 18, Edwards was the youngest player to compete at international level for England in the 20th century. His career, which promised to develop into one of the finest of all time, included 17 more appearances for England,

70

before it was brought tragically to an end by the Munich Air Disaster (*see 21 February*) ... Red Rum won his record third Grand National in **1977,** winning by 25 lengths from Churchtown Boy. **Charlotte Brew,** on Barony Fort, became the first woman to take part in the race ... Broadcasting lost one of its most distinctive voices in **1990** when BBC radio commentator **Peter Jones** died shortly after reporting on the Boat Race ... In **1993** the **Great Britain rugby league team beat France 72–6** at Swinton to establish a new Test record. Jonathan Davies also kicked a record ten goals in the match.

**3**

Snooker's answer to Mike Yarwood or Rory Bremner, **John Virgo,** was born in **1946.** A lengthy career at the top of world snooker has yielded him only one major title, the 1979 UK Championship. However, he is sought after for exhibition nights because of his entertaining act which includes mimicking his fellow players ... In **1988 David Llewellyn** shot a final round 65 in the AGF Biarritz Open to record a European Tour record low for 72 holes. His total of 258 beat the record of 259 set by Mark McNulty a year earlier. Llewellyn's fellow Welshman Ian Woosnam equalled the record with a 258 in the 1990 Torras Monte Carlo Open (*see 7 July*) ... **1993** was the first year in which the **Grand National** was not run, other than due to wartime stoppages. After a second false start, the organizers were unable to call the horses back. Several of them completed two circuits of the course and first over the line in the 'Grand National that wasn't' was Esha Ness, ridden by John White and trained by Jenny Pitman.

# APRIL

**4**

In **1892 West Bromwich Albion** beat Darwen 12–0 to record the biggest win in the first division of the Football League. The result was equalled by Nottingham Forest in 1909 when they beat Leicester Fosse by the same margin ... In **1930 Andrew Sandham** became the first man to score 300 runs in an innings in Test cricket. His total of 325 was compiled for England against the West Indies at Kingston, Jamaica ... The former world heavyweight boxing champion **Ernie Terrell** was born in **1939.** He is the tallest world heavyweight champion at 6 ft 6 in (1·98 m) ... On this day in **1981** an emotional moment in sporting history occurred at Aintree when **Bob Champion** won the Grand National on Aldaniti. Champion had been given only months to live after cancer was diagnosed in 1979. Against very long odds he beat the disease and so became the most celebrated Grand National winner in recent times. His mount, Aldaniti, was also a survivor, having overcome tendon trouble and a broken hock bone ... On the same day that Champion was winning the National in **1981, Susan Brown** was writing her name in the record books as the first woman to compete in the University Boat Race. She coxed the Oxford crew to an eight lengths victory over Cambridge.

**5**

**John Wisden,** the man who devised the famous *Wisden Cricketers' Almanack,* died on this day in **1884.** The first edition was published in 1864. It contained 116 pages and cost one shilling (5p) ... During the **Scotland versus England** match at Ibrox Stadium in **1902** part of a temporary wooden stand collapsed, killing 25 people and injuring hundreds more. A second tragedy struck the ground in 1971 (*see 2 January*) ... The first black world heavyweight boxing champion, **Jack Johnson,** lost his title on this day in **1915.** Conceding a massive height (5 inches/12·7 cm) and weight (25 pounds/11.3 kg) advantage to Jess Willard, he was knocked out in the 26th round of their scheduled 45-round contest in Havana, Cuba. It is the longest world heavyweight title fight under Queensberry Rules (*see 31 March*) . . . **Tom Finney,** one of the most versatile forwards to play for England, was born in **1922.** He was capped 76 times and twice received the Footballer of the Year award but domestic competition honours eluded him and his club Preston, where he stayed throughout his Football League career . . . **England** scored a then Test record 849 runs against the West Indies at Kingston in **1930,** thanks largely to Andrew Sandham's contribution of 325 runs (*see 4 April*). This occasion was the first on which any team had scored as many as 700 runs in a Test innings, let alone 800 . . . In **1947 Rangers beat Aberdeen 4–0** in front of 82,584 fans at Hampden Park to win the first Scottish League Cup final. They have since won it a record 18 times.

**6**

The **first modern Olympic Games,** the brainchild of Frenchman Baron Pierre de Coubertin, got underway at Athens on this day in **1896.** The opening ceremony at 2 p.m. was followed by the first events. The honour of winning the first Olympic gold medal went to the 27-year-old American triple jumper James Connolly. A total of 59 athletes from 10 nations took part in the Games, which lasted until 15 April . . . In **1900 James J. Jeffries** successfully defended his world heavyweight title by knocking out Jack Finnegan after just 55 seconds. It is the shortest world heavyweight contest on record.

**7**

In **1914 Al McCoy** knocked out George Chip in just 45 seconds to win the world middleweight title. It was the shortest world title fight on record until equalled by Lloyd Honeyghan in 1987 (*see 30 August*) ... The former Wales and British Lions rugby international **Cliff Morgan** was born in **1930.** He played for Wales 29 times and toured with the Lions in 1955. After a successful playing career he joined the BBC, at one time becoming head of radio outside broadcasting. He was also Henry Cooper's opposing captain on the first series of *A Question of Sport* ... On this day in **1968** the world of motor racing was devastated by the death of the great **Jim Clark,** who was killed while competing in a formula two race at Hockenheim. His Lotus-Cosworth spun off the track at 170 mph (273·5 km/hr) on the sixth lap and collided with a tree. The car disintegrated on impact, killing Clark outright. The Hockenheim circuit was later modified as a result of this accident ... At Headingley, Leeds, in **1990, Great Britain** suffered their first home defeat to France since 1967. They went down by 25–18 in the second rugby league Test match ... National Hunt jockey **Peter Scudamore** retired in **1993** after riding 1677 winners.

**8**

Norwegian ice skater, and later movie star, **Sonia Henie** was born in **1912.** She won the Olympic title in 1928, 1932 and 1936 and was world champion ten years in succession between 1927 and 1936. She turned professional in 1936 and made 10 films. She died in 1969 ... At Aintree in **1967,** Foinavon, ridden by John Buckingham, became the last 100–1 winner of the Grand National. He avoided a pile up at the 23rd fence, which caused most of the field to fall or refuse, to come home a comfortable winner ... **Nick Faldo** won his second successive US Masters title in **1990.** For the second year running the competition went to a play-off, Faldo again winning at the second extra hole, this time at the expense of the luckless Raymond Floyd. Faldo became the third consecutive British winner and only the second man, after Jack Nicklaus, to win the title back-to-back.

**9** Irish racehorse trainer **Vincent O'Brien** was born in **1917.** Successful both on the flat and over the jumps, he saddled winners of all the major Classics in England and Ireland, as well as other prestigious races such as the Prix de l'Arc de Triomphe and King George VI and Queen Elizabeth II Diamond Stakes. The best horse he ever trained was the 1970 Triple Crown winner Nijinsky ... **Severiano Ballesteros** was born in **1957.** One of the best golfers to come from mainland Europe, he first made his mark as a 19-year-old when he finished second to Johnny Miller in the 1976 British Open at Royal Birkdale. He emerged as the top money-winner in Europe and went on to win a record 60 events on the European Tour. He won the British Open in 1979 and in the following year took the US Masters title, regaining the latter in 1983. He won the British Open on two further occasions, in 1984 and 1988 ... In **1983 Jenny Pitman** became the first woman trainer to saddle a Grand National winner when Corbière, ridden by Ben de Haan, won at 13–1 ... In **1988** Southampton's **Alan Shearer** became the youngest person, at 17 years 240 days, to score a first-division hat-trick, against Arsenal.

**10** The first British world motor-racing champion **Mike Hawthorn** was born in **1929.** Less than six months after winning the title, in 1958, he was killed in a car crash in Surrey ... **Stan Mellor,** the former champion National Hunt jockey, was born in **1937.** Champion jockey three times between 1960 and 1962, he was also the first man to ride 1000 winners under National Hunt rules. Surprisingly, he never won the Grand National, Cheltenham Gold Cup or Champion Hurdle ... Top British sprinter **Linford Christie** was born in **1960.** Linford achieved his ultimate goal of winning the Olympic 100 metres title at Barcelona in 1992 ... In **1989 Nick Faldo** won his first US Masters title, beating Scott Hoch in a play-off at the second extra hole.

**11** Britain's leading female judo exponent, **Karen Briggs,** was born in **1963.** She won four world titles, all in the 48 kg (7 st) class, in 1982, 1984, 1986 and 1989 ... **Eight sendings off** in the Football League in **1992** took the season's total to 246, exceeding the previous record of 242 in 1982–83. The new edict on the 'professional foul' resulted in an increase in dismissals.

**12** **Leeds** became the first rugby league team to score 100 points when they beat Coventry 102–0 in **1913;** it remains the highest score for a league game ... **England** played their first soccer international at Wembley on this day in **1924,** drawing 1–1 with Scotland. Their first goal at the new stadium was scored by Billy Walker, who later managed two FA Cup winning teams at Wembley, Sheffield Wednesday in 1935 and Nottingham Forest in 1959 ... In **1930 Wilf Rhodes,** aged 52 years and 165 days, became the oldest man to play in a Test match for England.

The match, against the West Indies at Kingston, Jamaica, was Rhodes' 58th and last for England. Also making his last appearance for England on that day was **George Gunn,** aged 50 years and 320 days. They are the only two 50-year-olds to have played together in the same Test teams ... Former England soccer captain **Bobby Moore** was born in **1941.** He played for England a then-record 108 times and led the side on a record-equalling 90 occasions, the last time against Italy in November 1973. His greatest moment was to hold aloft the World Cup in 1966. In three successive years he skippered winning sides at Wembley; West Ham in the FA Cup in 1964, in the European Cup-winners' Cup in 1965, and England in 1966 (*see 24 February*) ... Boxing fans have mourned the loss of two of its great champions on this day. **Joe Louis,** who made a record 25 successful defences of the world heavyweight title, died in **1981;** and **'Sugar' Ray Robinson,** who died **1989.** (*see 3 and 13 May*).

# 13

In **1936 Joe Payne** set a Football League record by scoring ten goals for Luton Town in a third division (south) match against Bristol Rovers. He beat the previous record of nine, scored by Tranmere's 'Bunny' Bell less than four months earlier ... Chess champion **Gary Kasparov** was born in **1963.** He was only 22 years and 210 days when he beat the defending champion, Anatoly Karpov, in 1985 to become the youngest world champion ... **Severiano Ballesteros** became the youngest winner of the US Masters in **1980,** at 23 years and 4 days. He won by four strokes from American Gibby Gilbert and Australian Jack Newton ... At Jerez in **1986 Ayrton Senna,** in a Lotus, beat

Britain's Nigel Mansell, in a Williams, to win the Spanish Grand Prix. The win, by a mere 14/1000ths of a second, is the narrowest in formula one history.

**14** The most durable baseball player in the professional game, **Pete Rose,** was born in **1941.** He played in a record 3562 major league games, for Cincinnati, Philadelphia and Montreal, between 1963 and 1986 and scored 2165 runs. In 1989, however, while manager of the Cincinnati Reds, he was banned for life for betting on the outcome of his team's games. In the following year he was jailed for five months on a tax evasion charge ... Britain's best known and most successful male water skier, **Mike Hazelwood,** was born in **1958.** He won a record seven British titles between 1974 and 1983. In 1977 he became the first British winner of the overall world title. He also took the jumping world crowd, in 1979 and 1981 ... In **1991, Tottenham Hotspur** ended Arsenal's dreams of an FA Cup and League double by beating them 3–1 in the FA Cup semi-final, the first to be played at Wembley Stadium. When they met at the same stage two years later, Wembley was again used as the venue. This time Arsenal won ... The **first women's rugby World Cup final** was played in Cardiff in **1991.** The United States beat England 19–6.

**15** Snooker player **Joe Davis** was born in **1901.** The first to master the art of controlling the cue ball, he transformed snooker from a simple game of potting to one requiring great skill. He won the first world title in 1927 and went on to win it another 14 times before retiring from the championship in 1946; it is said he never lost a snooker match over level terms during his career. He also won the world professional billiards title four times. Joe died in 1978, a few months after collapsing while watching brother Fred's epic snooker world championship semi-final against South Africa's Perrie Mans ... In **1964 George Best** made his debut for Northern Ireland, and helped them to a 3–2 win over Wales at Swansea. It was the first of 37 caps for the Ulsterman, who scored nine goals for his country ... **Viv Richards** scored a century off just 56 balls against England at St John's in **1986.** No other cricketer has succeeded in scoring a century in so few balls. Australia's Jack Gregory holds the record for the shortest time taken to score a Test century. He took just 67 minutes to notch up 100 runs against South Africa in 1921 ... This date in **1989** was the blackest day in British sporting history when 95 soccer fans lost their lives in the **Hillsborough disaster** shortly after the start of the FA Cup semi-final between Liverpool and Nottingham Forest. The tragedy, and subsequent Taylor Report resulted in many changes to British soccer grounds with the ultimate aim of all-seater stadiums.

**16**

One of the best-known names in professional basketball, **Kareem Abdul-Jabbar,** was born in **1947.** Christened Lew Alcindor, he changed his name after converting to the Islamic faith in 1969. He played in a record 1560 National Basketball Association (NBA) games in a career that spanned 20 years, from 1970 to 1989. His tally of 38,387 points and 15,837 field goals are regular season records in the NBA. He also holds the record for post-season play-off games.

## 17

The **first international boxing match** took place at Farnborough, Hampshire, in **1860.** Tom Sayers of England met John C. Heenan of the United States in a bare-knuckle contest that ended in a draw after 37 rounds. Under the rules for such contests, a round ended when a fighter was knocked down ... In **1888** the **first formal meeting of the Football League** took place at the Royal Hotel, Manchester. It was attended by representatives of 12 clubs who agreed to form a League. The founder members were Accrington, Aston Villa, Blackburn Rovers, Bolton Wanderers, Burnley, Derby County, Everton, Notts County, Preston North End, Stoke, West Bromwich Albion and Wolverhampton Wanderers ... A British record crowd of 149,547 passed through the turnstiles at Hampden Park, Glasgow, in **1937** to watch the **Scotland versus England international.** It is estimated that a further 10,000 got in without paying ... Yachtswoman **Clare Francis** was born in **1946.** In 1976 she made the fastest crossing of the Atlantic by a woman. Competing in the *Observer* single-handed race, she made the crossing in 29 days ... **Riccardo Patrese,** the Italian motor-racing driver, was born in **1954 ... Neil Thomas** became the first Briton to win a medal in the World Gymnastics Championships when he took silver in the floor exercises of the tournament in **1993,** held at the National Exhibition Centre in Birmingham.

## 18

In **1903 Bury** registered the biggest winning margin in FA Cup final history by beating Derby County 6–0 at Crystal Palace ... Racing driver **Jochen Rindt** was born in **1942.** German-born, Rindt was brought up in Austria. In 1970 he became the first and only man to be declared world champion posthumously (*see 5 September*) ... West Indian fast bowler **Malcolm Marshall** was born in **1958**. He is only the second West Indian bowler, after Lance Gibbs, to take 300 Test wickets.

## 19

The **first Boston Marathon** was held in **1897** and won by John McDermott of New York. Held every April on Patriot's Day, it has been run every year since its inauguration and is the world's oldest annual race of its kind ... Test cricket umpire **Harold 'Dickie' Bird** was born in **1933**. A former player with Yorkshire and Leicestershire, he made his name as one of the best-known and best-loved umpires. ... The former England international footballer **Trevor Francis** was born in **1954**. He joined Birmingham City as a 16-year-old and subsequently transferred to Nottingham Forest, in 1979, becoming Britain's first £1 million footballer. He enjoyed a spell in Italy before returning to Britain and eventually going into management at Sheffield Wednesday ... **Bobby Charlton** played the first of his 106 games for England against Scotland at Hampden Park in **1958**. He also scored the first of his record 49 goals in the 4–0 win ... At St Mellion, Cornwall, in **1991, Ian Woosnam** missed the cut in the Benson and Hedges International after two opening rounds of 82; a week earlier he had won the US Masters. In the words of the immortal Greavsie: 'Funny 'ole game, golf!'

## 20

The **world's first motor race using mechanical power** took place at Paris in **1887**. Count Jules Philippe Albert de Dion won the 19·3-mile (31 km) race at an average speed of 37 mph

(59·5 km/hr) in his De Dion steam quadricycle ... **Phil Hill,** the first North American to win the world motor-racing drivers' title, was born in **1927.** He won the title in 1961 ... The former Great Britain rugby league coach **Maurice Bamford** was born in **1936.** He had unsuccessful periods at Huddersfield, Wigan and Batley before his talent as a motivator emerged at Halifax. He was snapped up by Leeds and then appointed coach to the national side ... In **1981 Steve Davis** won the first of his modern-day record six world professional snooker titles when he beat Welshman Doug Mountjoy 18–12 at Sheffield's Crucible Theatre.

## 21

At Filbert Street, Leicester, in **1930** 27,241 fans witnessed a 6–6 draw between **Leicester City and Arsenal,** a unique result in the first division of the Football League ... British tennis player **Angela Mortimer** was born in **1932.** She took the Wimbledon Ladies' title from fellow Briton Christine Truman in 1961 after losing the first set 6–4. It was the first all-British ladies' singles final since 1914 ... At Denial Bay, South Australia, in **1959, Alf Dean** landed a 2664 lb (1208 kg) great white shark. It measured 16 feet 10 inches (5·13 m) and is the largest fish ever caught on a rod.

## 22

Australian tycoon **Alan Bond** was born in **1938.** He was the man who masterminded Australia's win in the America's Cup in 1983 (*see 26 September*) ... **Alex Murphy,** one of the best known and most outspoken rugby league characters, was born in **1939.** He made his name as a player of outstanding ability with his hometown club, St Helens. He played for Great Britain

27 times and won most of the game's top honours. He went on to enjoy a successful, if not much-travelled, career as a coach. He also enjoyed a spell behind the BBC microphone as a rugby commentator ... On this day in **1959** the Crystal Palace goal-keeper **Vic Rouse** became the first fourth division player to win a full international cap. The occasion was not auspicious, however, and he conceded four goals in Wales's 4–1 defeat by Northern Ireland at Belfast ... British world champion boxer **Lloyd Honeyghan** was born in **1960.** Jamaica-born Hone-yghan beat Donald Curry to win the universal welterweight title in 1986. He lost the WBC version to Jorgé Vaca in 1987 but successfully regained it five months later ... In **1991** the former world junior-welterweight champion **Jack 'Kid' Berg** died at the age of 81.

**23**

The career of racing driver **Stirling Moss** ended in **1962** when he crashed his Lotus-Climax at 110 mph (177 km/h) during a hard-fought formula one race at Goodwood on Easter Monday. Hampered by a faulty gearbox, Moss was pushing hard to get back on terms with the race leader, Graham Hill, when he lost control. He recovered from a broken leg, broken ribs and serious head injuries, but did not race again in formula one (*see 6 August*) ... At the Crucible Theatre, Sheffield, in **1983** Canada's **Cliff Thorburn** recorded the first maximum 147 break in the world professional championship during his match against Terry Grif-fiths ... Former England cricketer **Jim Laker** died in **1986,** aged 63. His record of taking 19 wickets in one Test match still stands (*see 31 July*).

**24**

In 1741 **George Stevenson** became the first fighter to lose his life as a direct result of a prize fight. He died after a bout with Jack Broughton at Taylor's Booth, Tottenham Court Road, London (*see 16 August*) . . . In **1897 Batley beat St Helens 10–3** in front of 13,492 fans at Headingley, Leeds, to win the first Northern Union Cup (now the Rugby League Challenge Cup) . . . **Tommy Docherty,** the football manager reputed to have had more clubs than Jack Nicklaus, was born on this day in **1928.** In his playing days he was with Celtic and Preston North End, at the latter taking over the No. 4 shirt from Bill Shankly. Docherty enjoyed success as a manager at Chelsea and Manchester United, but also endured some failures, at Derby County and Wolverhampton Wanderers for example . . . Chorley's **Carl Crook** beat Najib Daho of Manchester in **1991** to retain his British lightweight title. This victory gave him a Lonsdale Belt in a record 161 days, beating the previous record of 203 days held by Robert Dickie since 1986 . . . **Gary Lineker** of Tottenham Hotspur received the Football Writers' Footballer of the Year Award for the second time in **1992;** he first won it in 1986, while at Everton. Other players to win the award twice are Tom Finney, Stanley Matthews, Kenny Dalglish and John Barnes.

**25**

One of the greatest all-round British sportsmen, **Charles Burgess ('C. B.') Fry,** was born in **1872.** In cricket he played for Sussex and Hampshire and was capped 26 times by England. He was an England soccer international and also appeared for Southampton in the 1902 FA Cup final. He played rugby union for the Barbarians. In 1893 he set a world long-jump record. He also managed to find time for politics and at three General

Elections stood as a Liberal Party candidate ... Dutch international footballer **Johan Cruyff** was born in **1947.** The backbone of the Dutch team that reached the 1974 World Cup final, he also steered his club Ajax to European Cup glory. He enjoyed a successful career in Spain with Barcelona, first as a player and later as a trainer, guiding them to a third successive Spanish league title in 1993 ... 'The Crafty Cockney', professional darts player **Eric Bristow,** was born in **1957.** He won the game's major titles, including a record five world professional darts championships ... On this day in **1964 Tranmere Rovers** took only four seconds from the kick-off to score against Bradford Park Avenue, a League record. The goal was credited to Jim Fryatt, although the claim is often disputed because three other players touched the ball before it entered the net, thus making four seconds seem unlikely.

**26**

The first female athlete to win four Olympic gold medals, **Fanny Blankers-Koen** of Holland, was born in **1918.** She won the four medals at the 1948 Olympics, in the 100 and 200 metres, the 80 metres hurdles, and the sprint relay ... The **1924** FA Cup final between **Newcastle and Aston Villa,** played on this day, was the first all-ticket FA Cup final (*see 28 April*) ... One of the BBC's top commentators, **David Coleman,** was born in **1926.** In recent years he has made a name for himself as the questionmaster on *A Question of Sport.*

**27**

The **1908 Olympics** opened at London's White City. A total of 2036 athletes from 23 nations took part in the Games which ended with the hosts topping the medals table with 145 medals, including 56 golds ... Meanwhile at Stamford Bridge in **1908, Manchester United and Queen's Park Rangers drew 1–1** in the first Charity Shield match. When the game was replayed four months later, United won 4–0 ... In **1956 Rocky Marciano** announced his retirement from boxing. He retired as the undefeated heavyweight champion of the world after 49 fights ... **Peter Scudamore** became the first National Hunt jockey to ride 200 winners in a season in **1989** when he partnered Gay Moore to victory at Towcester. It was the first double century by a British jockey since Gordon Richards rode 200 on the flat in 1952 ... **Ellery Hanley** skippered Wigan to a 13–8 victory over St Helens in the **1991** Rugby League Challenge Cup final at Wembley, becoming the first man in the history of the competition to captain his side to victory three years in succession.

**28**

**Bolton Wanderers and West Ham United** contested the first FA Cup final at Wembley in **1923.** Official receipts gave the attendance as 126,047 but it is estimated that more than 200,000 were in the ground (*see 26 April*). Bolton won 2–0, with David Jack having the honour of scoring the first goal ... Former England Test cricket captain **Mike Brearley** was born in **1942.** A great tactician and motivator, Brearley led Middlesex to four championships and two Gillette Cup victories between 1971–82. His record as England captain is phenomenal by present day standards: 18 Test wins out of a total of 31 played, with only four defeats ... Wigan's **Andy Gregory** became only the second Rugby League player to win the Lance Todd Trophy a second time. He was awarded this coveted laurel as man of the match for his contribution to Wigan's triumph over Warrington in the **1990** Challenge Cup final at Wembley. The only other player to win the trophy twice is Warrington's Gerry Helme. Gregory has the added bonus of making both his trophy-winning appearances at Wembley.

**29**

The **1933** FA Cup final between **Everton and Manchester City** was the first to see players wearing numbers on their shirts. The Everton players wore shirts numbered 1 to 11 while City wore numbers 12 to 22 ... Britain's best-known squash player, **Jonah Barrington,** was born in **1941.** He won the British Open championship six times between 1967 and 1974. The World Open title was inaugurated too late in Barrington's career for him to add it to his impressive list of tournament successes ... American golfer **Johnny Miller** was born in **1947.** He won the US Open in 1973 and the British Open at Birkdale in 1976 ... **Muhammad Ali** was stripped of his world heavyweight title in **1967** for refusing, on religious grounds, to be drafted into the US Army (*see 26 July*) ... **Chelsea beat Leeds United 2–1** after extra time at Old Trafford to win the replay of the **1970** FA Cup final, the first replay of a Wembley final ... The final of the **1989 Pilkington Cup** at Twickenham attracted a world record attendance for a rugby union club match of 59,300. Bath ran out 10–6 winners over Leicester ... In **1990 Stephen Hendry** beat Jimmy White 18–12 to become the youngest world snooker champion at the age of 21 years and 106 days (*see 13 January*) ... The **Law Society Legal Handicap Hurdle** at Hexham in **1991** saw a record-equalling seven horses start the race as co-favourites. Six of them filled the first six places.

**30**

The **Preston North End versus Huddersfield Town FA Cup** final in **1938** was the first to be televised in its entirety by the BBC. The viewers were treated to a thrilling game which was decided by a George Mutch penalty in the last minute of extra-time. All subsequent FA Cup finals have been shown live by the Corporation with the exception of the 1952 match between Newcastle and Arsenal; the Football Association refused permission for this to be televised ... **Lou Gehrig** set a major baseball league record in **1939** when he played his 2130th consecutive game for New York. His run of appearances stretched back to June 1925.

# MAY

**1** The first soccer international outside Great Britain was played by **Belgium and France** at Uccle, near Brussels, in **1904;** the teams drew 3–3 ... **Stirling Moss and co-driver Dennis Jenkinson** became the first British winners of the Mille Miglia in **1955,** in a Mercedes-Benz ... in **1958 Barcelona** won the first Inter-Cities Fairs Cup final, beating London 6–0 in the second leg ... American jockey **Steve Cauthen** was born in **1960.** After a successful career in the United States, including partnering Triple Crown winner Affirmed in 1978, Cauthen came to England. He won his first of three jockey's championships in 1984 and in the following year had his first success in the Epsom Derby, with Slip Anchor. Reference Point gave Cauthen his second victory in the race, in 1987 ... On this day in **1961 betting shops** became legal in Britain ... **Ben Lexcen,** designer of *Australia II*, the first non-American yacht to win the America's Cup (1983), died in **1988**.

**2** **Dr Benjamin Spock** was born in **1903.** Some 20 years before writing the best-selling *Common Sense Book of Baby and Child Care* (1946), Spock was a member of the US rowing eights gold medal team at the 1924 Paris Olympics ... **Stanley Matthews** finally won an FA Cup winner's medal in **1953** when Blackpool came from 3–1 behind to beat Bolton 4–3. Stan Mortensen became the third man, and the first in the 20th century, to score a hat-trick in a Cup final ... Snooker player **Jimmy White** was born in **1962.** Known as 'The Whirlwind', he was youngest-ever world amateur champion in 1980. He has appeared in five Embassy world professional snooker finals, but still awaits the win that his abundant talent deserves ... **Andy Gregory** made history in **1992** as the first man to win seven Rugby League Challenge Cup winners' medals when Wigan carried off the trophy for the fifth successive year.

**3**

Boxer '**Sugar' Ray Robinson**—real name Walker Smith—was born in Detroit in **1921.** He won the world welterweight title in 1946 and in 1951 took the middleweight crown. Only exhaustion prevented him winning a third title, light-heavyweight, when he retired in the 14th round against Joey Maxim in 1952. Robinson died in 1989 (*see 12 April*) . . . Another boxer was born on this day in **1934,** Britain's own **'Enery Cooper,** whose sporting behaviour and likable personality made him a great favourite with the general public. He is the only man to win three Lonsdale Belts outright. His only attempt at the world title resulted in a sixth-round stoppage by Muhammad Ali in 1966 . . . Czech gymnast **Vera Caslavska** was born in **1942.** She won seven Olympic gold medals; three in 1964 and four in 1968. She gave the medals won in 1968 to the four leading politicians in Czechoslovakia in a gesture of defiance against the Soviet invasion of her country . . . The one-time 'Golden Boy' of British golf, **Peter Oosterhuis,** was born in **1948.** Runner-up to Gary Player in the 1974 British Open, he later played mostly in the United States . . . Scottish athlete **Allan Wells** was born in **1952.** His greatest moment came at the Moscow Olympics in 1980 when he won the 100 metres gold medal . . . Also on this day in **1952, Newcastle beat Arsenal** to become the first team this century to win the FA Cup in successive seasons.

**4**

The **first Derby** was run at Epsom in **1780.** The name of the race was decided by a toss of the coin between the 12th Earl of Derby and Sir Charles Bunbury—the Epsom Bunbury would not have tripped off the tongue nearly so well. Bunbury had the consolation of seeing his horse, Diomed, partnered by jockey Sam Arnull, win the race ... **Peter Shilton** made his Football League debut in **1966,** playing for Leicester City against Everton. He has since gone on to play in more League games than any other man; his total was 968 at the start of the 1992–93 season ... In **1985 Wigan beat Hull 28–24** to win the Rugby League Challenge Cup final at Wembley. The points aggregate (52) is a record in the final of the competition.

**5**

Britain's most successful jockey, **Sir Gordon Richards,** was born in **1904.** He rode a record 4870 winners, including 14 Classic winners. Victory in the Derby came late in his career, after 27 failures. Days after receiving a knighthood from Her Majesty the Queen, in 1953, he rode 5–1 favourite Pinza to a four lengths win over the Queen's horse, Aureole. He rode 200 winners in a season a record 12 times and was champion jockey 26 times, between 1925 and 1953 ... In **1928** Everton centre-forward **'Dixie' Dean** went into the last match of the season, against Arsenal at Goodison Park, requiring three goals to beat George Camsell's record of 59 League goals in one season. His third goal came in the 82nd minute, when Dean rose to meet a corner and headed it into the net. The game ended 3–3, but Dean had set a new record ... The **1954** Rugby League Challenge Cup final replay between

**Warrington and Halifax** attracted the world's biggest rugby league crowd, 102,569, to Odsal Stadium, Bradford.

**6**

America's best-known horse race, the **Kentucky Derby,** was first run in 1875. The event is traditionally run over 1.25 miles (2 km) at Churchill Downs, Louisville, Kentucky, on the first Saturday in April. The inaugural winner was Aristides, ridden by Oliver Lewis ... In **1954 Roger Bannister** became the first man to run a mile in under four minutes; his exact time was 3 minutes 59·4 seconds. The world record came during a meeting between the AAAs and Oxford University at Iffley Road, Oxford. Bannister broke the four-minute barrier on only one other occasion subsequently ... Tottenham Hotspur beat Leicester City 2–0 in the **1961** FA Cup final at Wembley to become the first club this century to complete the League and Cup double ... In **1988 Worcestershire's Graeme Hick** set a 20th-century record by scoring 405 runs in a single innings, against Somerset at Taunton. His was the highest innings in Britain since 1895 when Lancashire's Archie MacLaren scored 424 on the same ground.

**7**

At Old Trafford in **1921** the second division game between **Stockport County and Leicester City** drew just 13 spectators, the lowest on record for a Football League match, although some sources reported a crowd in excess of 2000. The game was Stockport's last of the season, and relegation to the third division was already assured ... At The Oval in **1990 Lancashire** scored 863 runs in a county game against Surrey, only 24 runs short of the championship record set 94 years earlier. Neil Fairbrother scored 366 (*see 8 May*).

**8**

**Yorkshire** completed a record innings in the county cricket championship when they made 887 against Warwickshire at Edgbaston in **1896** ... The Surrey and England batsman **Jack Hobbs** completed his 100th first-class century on this day in **1923** ... Former world heavyweight boxing champion **Sonny Liston** was born in **1932**. He beat Floyd Patterson to take the title with a first-round knockout in 1962. He retained the title a year later, again by beating Patterson in one round, but met his match in newcomer Cassius Clay in 1964 (*see 25 February*). He suffered a first-round knockout by Clay (then Muhammad Ali) when trying to regain the title the following year. Liston died in 1970 (*see 30 December*) ... **Jackie Charlton,** a member of England's 1966 World Cup winning team, was born in **1936.** He played 629 League games for Leeds United between 1953 and 1973. He then went into management, immediately guiding Middlesbrough to the second-division title. He had spells at Newcastle and Sheffield Wednesday before taking over as manager of the Republic of Ireland team. He guided the national side to the finals of the European Championship and the World Cup for the first time in its history. Now one of Ireland's favourite sons, Jack spends what time he can away from football relaxing with a fishing rod in hand.

**9**

**Joe Davis** beat Tom Dennis 20–11 at Camkin's Hall, Birmingham, in **1927** to win the first world professional snooker championship. Davis beat a field of ten to take the trophy, which is still presented today. Davis' prize-money was just 10s 6d (52·5p) ... American tennis player **'Pancho' Gonzales** was born in **1928.** He won the US singles but never the Wimbledon title. However, at Wimbledon in 1969 he made history when he beat Charlie Pasarell in the longest-ever singles match. The contest went to 112 games (22–24, 1–6, 16–14, 6–3, 11–9) and took 5 hours 20 minutes to complete ... The former British boxing world champion **Terry Downes** was born in **1936.** He took the middleweight crown from the defending champion, Bostonian Paul Pender, in 1961 but lost it again, to the American, nine months later. His attempt to wrest the world light-heavyweight title from Willie Pastrano was brought to a halt in the 11th round at Manchester in 1964 ... Footballer **Bernard Joy** played his one and only game for England in **1936,** against Belgium. A member of the successful Corinthian Casuals team, he was the last amateur to play for England at this level.

**10**

On this day in **1886** the FA approved the giving of **caps** to players appearing in international matches. Contrary to popular belief, a cap is not awarded for every single international appearance. Each appearance in a friendly match is marked by the giving of a cap. Different rules apply for competitions, such as the World Cup or European Championship, where only one cap per tournament (including qualifying matches) is awarded. A cap given in these circumstances has the names of all the countries a player appeared against in the tournament sewn onto it . . . In **1980,** West Ham's **Paul Allen** became the youngest man to play in an FA Cup final. Aged only 17 years 256 days, he also became the youngest-ever recipient of a winner's medal after a goal from Trevor Brooking clinched the trophy for the second division side against favourites Arsenal.

## 11

One of Britain's most celebrated prize-fighters, **Tom Cribb,** died on this day in **1848.** Undefeated from 1805 until 1811, his two bouts with Tom Molineaux rate among the best contests seen in the days of bare-knuckle fighting . . . The former Newcastle United centre-forward **Jackie Milburn,** uncle of Bobby and Jack Charlton, was born in **1924.** He played for England 13 times and was a member of three FA Cup winning teams; he scored two goals in the 1951 final and one in 1955 (*see 9 October*) . . . Liverpool snooker player **John Parrott** was born in **1964.** He first made his presence felt in 1984 when he beat Alex Higgins and Tony Knowles before losing to Steve Davis in the semi-final of the Lada Classic. Parrott has gone on to become one of snooker's most consistent players. In 1990 he captured the world crown when he beat Jimmy White 18–12 at the Crucible Theatre, Sheffield. His previous appearance in the final, in 1989, had resulted in a resounding thrashing, 18–3 at the hands of Steve Davis . . . A crowd of 51,801 watched the **Crystal Palace v Burnley** second-division game at Selhurst Park in **1979.** It was the last time a current Football League club set its current record attendance (ground changes excepted) . . . A fire at the Valley Parade football ground, home of **Bradford City,** claimed the lives of 40 people in **1985.** The carnival atmosphere that greeted the new third-division champions for their last match of the season against Lincoln turned to terror and panic after 40 minutes when the main stand caught fire.

**12** Mayonaise won the **1859** One Thousand Guineas by 20 lengths, a record for a British Classic ... On this day in **1870** the first rules of **water polo** were drawn up by the London Swimming Association ... **Alan Ball,** the youngest member of England's 1966 World Cup team, was born in **1945.** He started his career with Blackpool and then moved to Everton in a six-figure transfer deal. His subsequent move to Arsenal for £220,000 made him the most expensive footballer in Britain. He later played for Southampton before venturing into management.

**13** One of the greatest heavyweight boxing champions, **Joe Louis,** was born in **1914.** Born Joseph Louis Barrow, he won the world heavyweight title in 1937 by beating James J. Braddock. He made a record 25 defences over 11 years, before retiring in 1948 after beating 'Jersey' Joe Walcott in New York. However, needing money to pay taxes, Louis came out of retirement two years later, losing on points over 15 rounds to the new champion, Ezzard Charles. Louis eventually retired for good after losing to Rocky Marciano in 1951. He died in 1981 (*see 12 April*) ... The first world motor-racing championship race took place at **Silverstone** in **1950.** Italy's Giuseppe Farina won the event, called the British Grand Prix, in an Alfa Romeo from teammate Luigi Fagioli. Farina went on to become the first world champion, beating Juan Manuel Fangio into second place.

**14** The oldest organized archery society, the **Yorkshire Society of Archers,** was formed in 1673 ... Golfing history was made on this day in 1754 when members of the **Society of St Andrews Golfers** played their first round over the St Andrews links. The Society was the forerunner of the R. & A. (Royal & Ancient) ... BBC Radio broadcast its **first cricket commentary** in 1927, the Rev. F.H. Gillingham commentating on the Essex versus New Zealand match from Leyton ... English-born yachtsman **Chay Blyth** was born in 1940 ... **Wakefield Trinity beat Hull 38–5** in the 1960 Rugby League Challenge Cup final to record the highest score ever made in the final ... In 1977 **Bobby Moore** played his last competitive match for second-division Fulham, away to Blackburn Rovers. He ended on a losing note, with the home side winning 1–0. On the same day in 1977 **Liverpool** became the first club to win the first division title ten times when they drew 0–0 at home to West Ham United. Liverpool went on to increase their number of titles to 18 ... **Wimbledon** announced in 1991 that they were moving from Plough Lane to Selhurst Park for the 1991–92 season.

**15** The **first baseball stadium** was opened at the Union Grounds, Brooklyn, on this day in 1862 ... Welsh world flyweight champion **Jimmy Wilde** was born in 1892. He was known as 'The Mighty Atom' because of the power he could pack for such a small man (*see 10 March*) ... **England** lost their first international soccer match outside the British Isles in 1929 when they were defeated 4–3 by Spain in Madrid ... The former England Test cricket captain **Ted Dexter** was born in 1935. He played first-class cricket for Cambridge University and Sussex and appeared for England 62 times. He is also an excellent golfer and has won the prestigious President's Putter competition at Rye . . . A piece of cricket history was made on this day in **1948: Australia** scored 721 runs against Essex at Southend-on-Sea, the largest total achieved in one day's play in a first class game . . . In **1963 Tottenham Hotspur** became the first British winners of a European trophy when they beat Atlético Madrid 5–1 to Rotterdam to take the Cup-winners' Cup. Jimmy Greaves scored two goals for Spurs.

## 16

**Olga Korbut,** the Soviet gymnast who captured hearts with her impish grin at the 1972 Olympics, was born in **1955.** She won three golds and a silver at Munich in 1972 and a gold and a silver four years later in Montreal. She later married Russian pop singer Leonid Bortkevich, the lead singer with the group Pesnyany . . . Playing for Surrey against the Australians at The Oval in **1956 Jim Laker** took all 10 wickets in an innings for 88 runs. He repeated the feat ten weeks later, but this time in the Old Trafford Test Match (*see 31 July*) . . . Argentine tennis player **Gabriela Sabatini** was born in **1970.** Her consistency in reaching the semi-final and finals of numerous tournaments has earned her prize-money in excess of $6 million. Her only Grand Slam singles title to date is the US Open which she won in two sets in 1990, beating Steffi Graf.

## 17

One of the best-known boxers of the modern era, **'Sugar' Ray Leonard,** was born in **1956.** The second man after Tommy Hearns to win world titles at five different weights, Leonard has won more prize-money than any other fighter outside the heavyweight division, with earnings in excess of $105 million. His bid for the undisputed welterweight crown, against Hearns in 1981, is reputed to have earned him $11 million. Leonard won his first world title in 1979 when he captured the WBC welterweight crown. He contested 12 world title fights and lost only one, on points to Roberto Duran at Montreal in 1980.

**18** **Fred Perry,** the last Briton to win the Wimbledon men's singles title, was born in **1909.** Perry won three Wimbledon titles consecutively, 1934–36. He was the first man to win the singles titles of all four Grand Slam events. A designer of quality sportswear bearing his name, he is also a member of the BBC's tennis commentary team ... **Nobby Stiles,** that 'toothless' member of the England World Cup winning squad, was born in **1942.** He made his name as a tough-tackling defender with Manchester United and England, and was one of the game's great characters ... In **1950 Jimmy Mullen** became England's first substitute in a football international, coming on for Jackie Milburn against Belgium in Brussels. He went on to score and thus became the first sub to score in an international ... In **1960 Real Madrid** gave a devastating display of attacking football to win the European Champions' Cup for the fifth consecutive year. They capped their domination of the competition with a 7–3 demolition job on Eintracht Frankfurt in front of 127,000 fans at Hampden Park, Glasgow. Alfredo di Stefano (three goals) and Ferenc Puskas (four goals) were the hitmen for the Spanish side, served superbly by their team-mates in midfield. The match is still talked about by football fans, who never seem to tire of reliving on film its many magic moments ... **Roberto Baggio** was transferred from Fiorentina to Juventus for a then world record £7·7 million in **1990.**

**19**

In **1965 Bobby Moore** captained West Ham to a memorable European Cup-winners' Cup triumph over Munich 1860 at Wembley. The Hammers won thanks to a pair of goals by Alan Sealey. It was the second leg of a great hat-trick for Moore, who led West Ham to victory over Preston in the 1964 FA Cup final and, of course, in 1966, he made it three successive trips up the famous Wembley steps when he led England to victory in the 1966 World Cup final ... **Liverpool** enjoyed European glory on this day in **1976** when they drew 1–1 at FC Bruges in the second leg of their UEFA Cup tie. The score-line was good enough to give them an overall 4–3 victory on aggregate. The club won the European Champions' Cup the following year, beating Borussia Moenchengladbach 3–1, and in 1978 joined the ranks of the select few clubs that have retained the trophy by beating FC Bruges 1–0 at Wembley ... In **1984** Liverpool's neighbours, **Everton,** beat Elton John's Watford, making their first appearance, to win the FA Cup, winning the trophy for the fourth time. The Toffees (Everton) were making the first of three successive Wembley appearances in the final, a record equalled only by Arsenal.

**20**

**Bobby Charlton** scored his 49th and last goal for England, against Colombia at Bogota, in a warm-up game for the **1970** World Cup in Mexico. His tally still stands as a record; Gary Lineker came to within one of it when he played his last game for England in 1992 ... **Monica Seles** ended Steffi Graf's record of 66 consecutive victories when she beat her in the final of the **1990** BMW German Open in Berlin; Seles won 6–4, 6–3 ... Third time lucky **Barcelona** won the European Cup in **1992,** with Ronald Koeman scoring the only goal of the match, against Sampdoria at Wembley, in extra time. In their two previous appearances in the final the Catalan side had lost 3–2 to Benfica, in 1961, and 2–0 on penalties to Steaua Bucharest, in 1986, when Terry Venables was in charge.

## 21

Delegates from seven countries formed **FIFA** (Fédération Internationale de Football Association) at a meeting in Paris in **1904.** The founder members were Belgium, Denmark, France, Holland, Spain, Sweden and Switzerland. Today more than 160 nations belong to the organization ... **Henry Cooper's** dream of taking the world heavyweight crown was dashed in **1966** when a cut eye put paid to his challenge to champion Muhammad Ali at Highbury football stadium. The two boxers were level on points at the time of the stoppage, in the 6th round. Henry's age-old problem of cutting easily let him down during the most crucial bout of his career. The fight was the first world heavyweight contest in London since Tommy Burns beat Jack Palmer in 1908 at the Wonderland Centre.

## 22

One of the world's most talented footballers, **George Best,** was born in **1946.** Best is rated second only to Pelé by the game's leading experts. He was temperamental, which caused difficulties on and off the pitch, but such exceptional talent rarely comes without this drawback. He made his debut for Manchester United at the age of 17, and after just 15 League games gained the first of his 37 caps for Northern Ireland. The beginning of the end of his career at United coincided with the departure of manager Sir Matt Busby. In January 1974 Best walked out on the club for good after making 466 appearances and scoring 178 goals. He subsequently showed his talents at a less exalted level, firstly at Stockport County, then across the Atlantic, before returning to the British Isles to play for Fulham, Hibernian, Motherwell, Cork Celtic, Bournemouth and various non-league clubs. Among the many brilliant goals Best scored for United one of the very best came in the 1968 European Cup final against Benfica at Wembley. The teams were level at 1–1 when, in a typical burst of daring and breathtaking ball control, Best sidestepped the defenders and rounded the 'keeper to make it 2–1 and set up United's great victory ... **Wembley Stadium** went all-seater in **1990** for the England versus Uruguay friendly. Only 38,751 people bothered to turn up to see England's first home defeat in six years.

**23** Cricket's Brylcreem boy of the 1950s, **Denis Compton,** was born in **1918.** He made his debut for Middlesex in 1936 and during a 28-year career in first-class cricket scored nearly 39,000 runs. He played for England 78 times, scoring 5807 runs. His greatest achievements came in the 1947 season when he scored a remarkable record-breaking 3816 runs, including a record 18 centuries. His Middlesex colleague Bill Edrich managed 3539 runs, the second highest tally in a season, as Middlesex, hardly surprisingly, won the championship. Denis played soccer for Arsenal, as did his brother Leslie, and won an FA Cup winner's medal with the side in 1950. Both also played soccer for England, although Denis only appeared in a wartime international... **Anatoly Karpov,** the Soviet world chess champion, 1975–85, was born in **1951.** He won 26 of the 32 tournaments he played during his reign as world champion ... Former world middleweight boxing champion **Rocky Graziano** died, aged 68, in **1990.** The subject of the Paul Newman film *Somebody Up There Likes Me,* Graziano took the title in 1947 by beating Tony Zale in Chicago. He lost his title to Zale 11 months later and in 1952 failed in a second attempt to regain it when 'Sugar' Ray Robinson knocked him out in the third round.

## 24

In **1877** the **MCC and Ground cricket team dismissed Oxford University** for 12 runs at Oxford. The total remains the lowest for a first-class innings, although this unenviable record was later shared by Northants in 1907 (*see 11 June*). Oxford batted one man short ... French tennis star **Suzanne Lenglen,** the first non-English speaking winner of the Wimbledon ladies singles, was born in **1899.** She won the first of her six Wimbledon singles titles in 1919 and in the process caused a stir with her grace and athleticism. The loose, short-length dress she wore revolutionized fashion in the ladies' game. Five of her six titles were won in consecutive years, 1919–23. She also won six doubles and three mixed doubles titles, giving her a then-record of 15 Wimbledon titles ... At Inchmurrin, Strathclyde, in **1984** Alan Pettigrew set a world record by throwing a haggis 180 feet 10 inches (55·1 m).

## 25

**Jesse Owens** set six world records in 45 minutes at Ann Arbor, Michigan, in **1935.** One of them, the long jump, stood for 25 years. Owens reckoned he was suffering from a bad back at the time! (*see 12 August*) ... At Lewiston, Maine, in **1965 Muhammad Ali** made short work of his first challenger for the world heavyweight crown, knocking out ex-champion Sonny Liston in the first round. The crowd of 2434 is the smallest recorded at a world heavyweight contest ... In **1967 Glasgow Celtic** became the first British club to win the European Cup when they beat a dull Inter Milan side 2–1 in Lisbon ... Ten years to the day later, **Liverpool** won the trophy for the first time, beating Borussia Moenchengladbach 3–1 in Rome. Liverpool have won the trophy four times, a British record.

## 26

Football's **Matt Busby** was born in **1909.** He took over as manager of Manchester United in 1945 and led them to three League titles before the Munich air crash in 1958 destroyed the team he had so carefully nurtured and of which all football enthusiasts had such high hopes. He came back from this tragedy, leading a rebuilt United team to further League success and eventually, in 1968, to an historic win in the European Cup, the first by an English club ... In **1927 André Lagache and René Leonard** drove a Chenard and Walcker to victory in the first Le Mans 24-hour race at an average speed of 57.21 mph (92 km/hr) ... South African athlete **Zola Budd** was born in **1966.** The bare-foot runner was at the centre of two controversies in 1984. The first controversy arose when the *Daily Mail* newspaper orchestrated a campaign to enable her to compete in the Los Angeles Olympics. Budd was given a passport in double-quick time and was selected for the British Olympic team. The second controversy arose in the final of the 3000 metres in LA and a showdown with Mary Decker, whose world record in the 5000 metres Budd had beaten earlier in the year (*see 10 August*) ... **Norman Whiteside** became the youngest person, at 18 years and 18 days, to score in an FA Cup final, in **1983.** He scored for Manchester United in their replay against Brighton at Wembley. United, who had been held to a 2–2 draw by the southern underdogs on 21 May, won emphatically 4–0 ... **Arsenal** snatched the first-division title from Liverpool in almost the last kick of the season in **1989.** One goal up going into the final minute of the game against their great Merseyside rivals, Arsenal required at least a two-goal margin to give them the title on goal difference. Michael Thomas obliged, depriving Liverpool of a Cup and League double ... On this day in **1992** the on-off deal between Tottenham and Italian club Lazio for the services of **Paul Gascoigne** was finally completed.

**27**

American golfer **Sam Snead** was born in **1912.** Snead holds the record for the number of wins on the US Tour (81). He won the US Masters three times, the PGA three times and the British Open once, in 1946. He never captured the US Open, although he came close several times. In 1965, aged 52 years and 10 months, he became the oldest winner on the US Tour ... Liverpool boxer **John Conteh** was born in **1956.** He beat Jorgé Ahumada in 1974 to become the first British world light-heavyweight champion since Freddie Mills ... **Fiorentina beat Rangers 2–1** in the second leg of the first European Cup-winners' Cup final in Milan in **1961.** The Italian club took the trophy 4–1 on aggregate ... On this day in **1964 Fred Pickering** became the last man to score a hat-trick on his England debut. His team beat the United States 10–0 ... The 1987 Wimbledon champion **Pat Cash** was born in **1965.** The first Australian winner of the tournament since John Newcombe in 1971, Cash has struggled to find his form since his straight sets win over Ivan Lendl in the final ... England international footballer **Paul Gascoigne** was born in **1967.** He played for Newcastle and Tottenham before a £5·5 million move to Italian side Lazio in 1992 ... **1987** New Zealand recorded the highest score in the Rugby Union World Cup, beating Fiji 74–13 at Christchurch.

## 28

The **first TT race** on the Isle of Man took place in **1907.** One race was held over 10 laps of the St John's Circuit. The single-cylinder category was won by Charlie Collier on a Matchless travelling at an average speed of 38·20 mph (61·4 km/hr). 'Rem' Fowler won the twin-cylinder category on a Norton ... Super-star **Diego Maradona** moved from Argentinos Juniors to Barcelona in **1982** in soccer's first £5 million transfer ... **Maiden,** skippered by Tracy Edwards, and with an all-girl crew, sailed into Southampton at the end of the Whitbread Round the World Yacht race in **1990.** The yacht finished a commendable 18th overall.

## 29

In **1902 Edgbaston** became the fifth English Test cricket ground. England celebrated by bowling out Australia for just 36 runs ... German showjumper **Alwin Schockemöhle** was born in **1935.** He won the 1976 Olympic title on Warwick Rex.

His brother Paul was also a top international showjumper . . . Leading National Hunt trainer **Martin Pipe** was born in **1945.** His horses won a record 230 races in the 1990–91 season and collected a record £1.2 million prize-money. Many of Pipe's winners have been ridden by Peter Scudamore . . . **Sir Edmund Hillary and Sherpa Tenzing** became the first men to reach the summit of Mount Everest, at 11·30 a.m. on 29 May **1953** . . . Two goals from **Bobby Charlton** helped Manchester United beat Benfica 4–1 after extra time in **1968** to become the first English winners of the European Cup . . . In **1974 Alan Old** scored 37 points for the British Lions against South Western Districts at Mossel Bay, South Africa, a tour record by a Lions player. Team-mate J. J. Williams also made the record books, scoring a tour record six tries . . . A riot at the **Heysel Stadium,** Brussels, in **1985** resulted in 41 Italian and Belgian football fans losing their lives as a wall and safety fence collapsed before the start of the European Cup final between Liverpool and Juventus. Juventus won the match 1–0 (*see 2 June*).

**30**

**Ray Harroun,** in a Marmon Wasp, won the inaugural Indianapolis 500 race in **1911.** The event is staged annually at the end of May as part of the Memorial Day celebrations . . . Former England fast bowler and Test cricket captain **Bob Willis** was born in **1949.** His finest hour came in the 1981 Headingley Test when he prevented Australia from scoring the 130 runs they needed to win with a devastating spell that produced eight wickets for 43 runs . . . In **1971 Keith Boyce** of Essex enjoyed one of his best spells when he took eight Lancashire wickets for 26 runs to set a John Player Sunday League record.

**31**

The **first recorded bicycle race** took place over a two-kilometre (1.25 miles) course at the Parc de St Cloud in **1868** and was won by James Moore of Britain ... In **1965 Jim Clark** of Britain became the first non-American winner of the Idianapolis 500, winning in his Lotus at an average speed of 150·69 mph (242·4 km/hr) ... In **1980 Tony Ward** scored 18 points against South Africa at Cape Town, a record for a British Lions' player in an international ... Former world heavyweight boxing champion **Jack Dempsey** died in **1983** (*see 24 June*) ... In **1984** West Indian batsman **Viv Richards** set a record in a one-day international, scoring 189 not out against England at Old Trafford.

# JUNE

# JUNE

**1**

**Trent Bridge** became the fourth English Test cricket ground in 1899 when it hosted the England v Australia Test ... The **BBC broadcast its first commentary of the Epsom Derby** on this day in **1927.** The race was won by Call Boy, ridden by Charlie Elliott ... **Gordon Richards** was knighted by Her Majesty the Queen in **1953.** Sir Gordon showed his gratitude six days later by beating the Queen's horse, Aureole, into second place in the Derby! (*see 5 May*) ... Britain's top chess player **Nigel Short** was born in **1965.** The highest ranked Briton ever on the Elo list (the accepted rating system for chess-playing ability), he came through the eliminators to earn a meeting with defending world champion Gary Kasparov in 1993 ... **Lester Piggott** rode his record ninth Derby winner, Teenoso, on this day in **1983.**

**2**

Swimmer **Johnny Weissmuller** was born in **1904.** The first man to swim 100 metres in under one minute, he won five gold medals at the 1924 and 1928 Olympics (*see 20 January*) ... **Lester Piggott** won his first Epsom Derby in **1954** at the age of 18, partnering 33–1 shot Never Say Die to a memorable win. His mount was the first American-bred winner since Iroquois in 1881. Piggott went on to ride a record nine Epsom Derby winners. Two weeks after his Derby triumph he was suspended for six months for his reckless riding of the same horse at Royal Ascot and so missed the chance of riding him in the St Leger. Charlie Smirke got the ride and won the race ... The former racing driver, and later top manufacturer, **Bruce McLaren** of New Zealand was killed in **1970** while testing one of his own Can-Am cars at Goodwood ... In **1985** UEFA ruled that

**English football clubs** would be banned indefinitely from playing in Europe following the riot at the Heysel stadium, for which Liverpool fans were held responsible (*see 29 May*) ... **Didier Camberabero** scored a record 30 points in France's 70–12 win over Zimbabwe in the **1987** Rugby Union World Cup at Auckland.

**3**

In **1899 W. G. Grace** became the first man to play Test cricket beyond the age of 50. He was 50 years and 320 days old at the time of the Test between England and Australia in that year, the third oldest man to appear in a Test match ... The **Ryder Cup** was inaugurated on this day in **1927** when teams from the United States and Great Britain met at Worcester, Massachusetts. After two days of play the United States had won the foursomes 3–1 and the singles $6\frac{1}{2}$–$1\frac{1}{2}$ to win the match by seven points ... **BBC television transmitted the Epsom Derby** for the first time in **1931.** Freddie Fox rode Cameronian to victory ... American golfer **Hale Irwin** was born in **1945.** His $4 million plus earnings on the US Tour includes three wins in the US Open, in 1974, 1979 and 1990. He was aged 45 years 15 days at the time of his third win, making him the tournament's oldest winner ... The Aga Khan's **Shergar** won the Epsom Derby by a record 10 lengths in **1981.** He was kidnapped from his yard in Ireland two years later (*see 8 February*) ... In **1991 Tommy ('The Hitman') Hearns** beat Virgil Hill to win the WBA light-heavyweight crown. It was his sixth title at a different weight ... Also in **1991, Brian Bevan,** the most prolific try-scorer in rugby league history, died at the age of 66 (*see 22 February*).

**4** **Emily Davison** was fatally injured while trying to draw attention to the suffragettes' cause by grabbing hold of the reins of the King's horse Anmer in the **1913** Derby as it rounded Tattenham Corner at full gallop. Davison died from her injuries four days later. The race was won by Aboyeur ... National Hunt jockey **Bob Champion** was born in **1948.** Given only eight months to live after cancer was diagnosed in 1979, he won the 1981 Grand National (*see 4 April*) ... The **British Lions** rugby union team notched up their biggest Test win in **1966,** beating Australia 31–0 at Brisbane ... **Ed Moses** lost more than a race when Danny Harris pipped him at Madrid in **1987.** This defeat ended the longest winning streak in track history, 122 hurdles victories stretching back to August 1977.

**5** The **1938** World Cup match between **Brazil and Poland** at the Stade de la Mainau, Strasbourg, was remarkable for being the first in the final stages of the competition in which two players each scored four goals. Leonidas of Brazil scored his fourth goal three minutes into extra time to become the first man to score four goals in the World Cup. Fifteen minutes later Ernst Wilimowski of Poland scored *his* fourth to become the second man. The final score was 6–5 to Brazil ... In **1968 Alan Mullery** had the dubious distinction of being the first man to be sent off while playing for England in a full international, against Yugoslavia in the European Championships at Florence. Yugoslavia won the game 1–0.

**6** In **1727 James Figg** beat Ned Sutton in what is believed to be the first bare-knuckle boxing contest to have a title at stake ... The **first soccer international** between a British team and foreign opposition took place in Vienna in **1908.** England beat Austria 6–1. ... Irish rugby international **Willie John McBride** was born in **1940.** He played for Ireland 63 times and for the British Lions a record 17 times on five tours. In 1974 he guided Ireland to their first outright championship title since 1951 ... Swedish lawn-tennis ace **Bjorn Borg** was born in **1956.** He won the French Open six times and the Wimbledon singles title a modern-day record five years in succession. Borg was the youngest Wimbledon champion for 45 years when, aged 20, he won his first title in 1976. The US Open was the only major championship title to elude him. Borg retired in January 1983 but has since made several unsuccessful comebacks (*see 5 July*) ... Middlesex and England cricketer **Mike Gatting** was born in **1957.** Appointed England captain in 1986, he led a successful tour of Australia in 1987. The 1987/88 winter tour to Pakistan was soured by a controversy over umpiring decisions, and led to Gatting's dismissal as captain. He lost his place in the full England team as a consequence of leading a rebel England side to South Africa in 1990, but earned a recall for the 1992–93 tour of India.

**7** At Northampton in **1957 Micky Stewart** of Surrey created a record in first-class cricket by becoming the first outfielder to take seven catches in an innings, against Northants. Stewart later went on to become the England cricket manager ... In **1970** Derbyshire bowler **Alan Ward** earned a place in the record books for dismissing four Sussex batsmen in four balls in the John Player Sunday League ... In the **1989** Epsom Derby, 500–1 shot Terimon, ridden by Michael Roberts, finished second to the favourite Nashwan to become the highest priced horse to be placed in the race. The only other horse to finish in the first three at odds of more than 100–1 was the 200–1 shot Black Tommy in 1857 ... Newly promoted **Swindon Town** were relegated from the first division to the third of the Football League in **1990** after admitting to 35 breaches of rules on irregular payments to players. However, on appeal they were allowed to stay in the second division, a decision which upset Tranmere who as a consequence had to stay in the third division.

**8**

The former England cricket captain **Ray Illingworth** was born in **1932.** He spent most of his career with his native Yorkshire but ended it at Leicestershire. He captained both sides, and played for England 61 times. His son Richard, a bowler like his father, made his England debut against the West Indies in 1991 ... Spin bowler **Derek Underwood** was born in **1947.** He had an outstanding career with Kent, taking 2465 wickets between 1963 and 1987. He took 297 wickets in 86 Test appearances for England ... **Barry McGuigan** ended the Panamanian Eusebio Pedroza's seven-year reign as WBA featherweight champion in **1985.** The Irishman won on points to become the first UK holder of the featherweight title since Howard Winstone in 1968 ... The opening game of the **1990** World Cup produced a shock for defending champions **Argentina** who were beaten 1–0 by Cameroon in front of 73,780 fans at the Giuseppe Meazza stadium in Milan.

**9**

In **1899** the first British-born heavyweight champion of the world, **Bob Fitzsimmons,** was defeated in 11 rounds by James J. Jeffries at Coney Island, New York. Fitzsimmons had held the title for two years. He failed to regain it when he fought Jeffries again in 1902. The next British world heavyweight champion would be Lennox Lewis, in 1993 ... **Monica Seles,** at 16 years and 6 months, became the youngest winner of a Grand Slam tournament since Lottie Dod (*see 24 September*) in 1887 when she beat Steffi Graf 7–6, 6–4 in the final of the French Open at Roland Garros in **1990** ... The first all-American French Open final since Trabert and Larsen in 1954 took place a year later, in **1991**, when **Jim Courier** beat Andre Agassi in five sets.

**10**

The **first Oxford versus Cambridge Boat Race** took place in **1829,** raced over a course from Hambledon Lock to Henley Bridge; Oxford won. The modern race is rowed over 4 miles 374 yards (c. 7 km) from Putney to Mortlake ... On this day in **1907** drivers in the world's **first long-distance car race** set off from Peking for Paris (*see 10 August*) ... England soccer player **David Platt** was born in **1966.** He started his career with Crewe and then moved to Aston Villa. He was transferred to the Italian club Bari for £5·5 million in 1991. He has since moved to the crack Italian club Juventus ... **Al Geiberger** became the first man to shoot a sub-60 round on the US Tour when in **1977** he recorded a 59 in the Danny Thomas Golf Classic at the Colonial Golf Course, Memphis, Tennessee. Chip Beck equalled his record in 1991 (*see 12 October*) ... In **1981 Sebastian Coe** ran the 800 metres in a time of 1 minute 41·73 seconds at Florence,

Italy. The time was still a world record in August 1993 . . . Under captain Graham Gooch, **England beat the West Indies** by 115 runs in the first Test at Headingley in **1991** to record their first home win against the tourists since 1969.

## 11

Northamptonshire were bowled out by **Gloucestershire** for 12 runs at Gloucester in **1907** to equal the lowest first-class cricket innings set in 1877 (*see 24 May*) . . . One of the best-known female cricketers and former captain of the England team, **Rachael Heyhoe Flint,** was born in **1939.** She led the England ladies' team in 25 Tests between 1960 and 1979 and scored a record 1814 runs. Her achievements helped to popularize the ladies' game . . . Born on the same day as Rachael in **1939** was the former world motor-racing champion **Jackie Stewart.** The popular Scot was world champion in 1969, 1971 and 1973. His 27 wins from 99 starts stood as a record until beaten by Alain Prost in 1987 . . . Racehorse trainer **Jenny Pitman** was born in **1946.** She became the first woman to saddle a Grand National winner when Corbière won at 13–1 in 1983 . . . In **1952 Denis Compton** hit the 100th century of his first-class career. He had increased his tally to 123 by the time of his retirement in 1964 . . . On this day in **1953 Len Hutton** became England's first professional cricket captain . . . **Europe's worst-ever motor-racing disaster** occurred on this day in **1955** during the Le Mans 24-hour race. The Mercedes of Pierre Levegh left the track after clipping the Austin Healey of Lance Macklin at over 150 mph (240 km/hr) and somersaulted into the crowd, killing 83 people—including Levegh—and injuring about 100 . . . Top bowls player **Tony Allcock** was born in **1955.**

## 12

In **1930** in New York **Max Schmeling** of Germany became the first and only man to *win* the world heavyweight title on a disqualification. His opponent, American Jack Sharkey, was disqualified in the fourth round after committing a foul . . . The former Tottenham, Arsenal and Northern Ireland goalkeeper **Pat Jennings** was born in **1945.** He started his career at Watford and went on to become the first British player to appear in 1000 first-class matches. He played in goal for Northern Ireland 119 times, a UK record until surpassed by England 'keeper Peter Shilton.

## 13

What is regarded as the **first 'real' motor race** ended on this day in **1895.** The first car to cross the line in the Paris-Bordeaux-Paris race was a Panhard-Levassor driven by Emile Levassor at an average speed of 15 mph (24 km/hr) . . . One of the greatest long-distance runners of all-time, **Paavo Nurmi,** was born in **1897.** The Finn won a record 12 medals, including nine golds, in the three Olympics between 1920 and 1928 . . . **Donald Budge,** the first man to achieve a Grand Slam in tennis, was born on this day in **1915.** He performed the Grand Slam in 1938, the year in which he won the Wimbledon title for the second successive year . . . The **Isle of Man TT races,** held between 11 and 13 June, were dubbed the 'British Grand Prix' in **1949.** The three races, at 500, 350, and 250 cc, became the first races in the newly instituted world motor-cycling championships . . . **Tony Knowles,** snooker's pin-up boy, was born in **1955** . . . **Real Madrid beat Stade de Rheims 4–3** in Paris in **1956** to win the first European Cup . . . Jockey **Peter Scudamore** was born in **1958.** The first National Hunt jockey to ride 200 winners in a season (1989), he was champion jockey seven years in succession (1986–92). His total of more than 1500 winners makes him the most successful jump jockey of all-time.

## 14

The first **Henley Regatta** on the Thames was started in **1839.** Enthusiasts of rowing regard the event as a showcase for their sport, but in the public imagination it ranks with Ascot as an occasion for strawberries, champagne, top hats and expensive frocks. The chief event, the Grand Challenge Cup, remains one of the two most important races rowed over the c. $1\frac{1}{4}$-mile (2 km) course. The other, the Diamond Sculls, was first run in 1884. . . . **Steffi Graf,** the girl who took over the mantle of the top woman tennis player from Martina Navratilova, was born in **1969.** German-born Steffi has won all four Grand Slam titles, including Wimbledon five times. Her first Grand Slam was achieved in 1988 . . . At Old Trafford in **1979 Canada** recorded the lowest completed innings in cricket's World Cup competition history when they were dismissed by England for just 45 runs.

## 15

**Hungary beat El Savador 10–1** at Elche, Spain, in **1982** to register the highest score in the final stages of the soccer World Cup. Three-nil up at the interval, Hungary added seven goals in the second half to become the first team to score ten goals in a match in the final stages of the tournament. Three of the goals were scored by Laszlo Kiss, who came on for Hungary in the 55th minute. He was the first sub to score a hat-trick in the final stages of the competition.

**16**

One of England's most elegant batsmen, **Tom Graveney,** was born in **1927.** He scored 47,793 first-class runs between 1948 and 1971. In 79 Test appearances he scored 4882 runs ... The first four places in the **1929 Le Mans 24-Hour race** were occupied by British-made Bentleys. The pairing of Woolf Barnato and Sir Henry Birkin took first place, their car averaging 73·63 mph (118·4 km/h) ... In **1932** Yorkshire's first wicket partnership of **Herbert Sutcliffe and Percy Holmes** established a new record during the match against Essex at Leyton. Their partnership ended after 555 runs when Sutcliffe was dismissed for 313 runs. Holmes remained unbeaten on 224. The partnership beat the previous 34-year-old record by one run. It was surpassed by West Indians Frank Worrell and Clyde Walcott in the 1945–46 season ... The world's most successful motor cyclist, **Giacomo Agostini** of Italy, was born in **1942.** He won more world titles (15) and more world championship races (122) than any other man. He won the coveted 500cc title a record eight times between 1966 and 1975 ... Panamanian boxer **Roberto Duran** was born in **1951.** Known as 'Stone Fists', he won the WBA lightweight title in 1972 when he stopped Britain's Ken Buchanan. He relinquished the title in 1979 to concentrate on the welterweight division. He then beat 'Sugar' Ray Leonard for the welterweight crown. He went on to win world titles at junior-middleweight and middleweight ... In **1982** England midfield supremo **Bryan Robson** scored in just 27 seconds against France at Bilbao; the goal is the quickest in World Cup history.

**17** Former England pace bowler **Brian Statham** was born in 1930. He spearheaded, with Freddie Trueman, the England attack in the 1950s. He played for England 70 times and took 252 Test wickets ... Another top sportsman of the 1950s has a birthday today. Athlete **Derek Ibbotson** was born in 1932. The first man to run the mile in *exactly* four minutes, he won back the world mile record for Britain at the White City in 1957, beating Australian John Landy's record with a time of 3 minutes 57·2 seconds ... The world's best known and most successful cyclist, **Eddy Merckx,** was born in 1945. He won the Tour de France a record-equalling five times and also the other major 'Tours', of Italy and Spain. He was world professional road race champion three times ... In 1971 **David Duckham** became the first man to score six tries in a tour match for the British Lions, against West Coast-Buller at Greymouth, New Zealand ... **Norman Whiteside** became the youngest player to compete in the final stages of the World Cup, in 1982. He was 17 years 41 days when he appeared for Northern Ireland against Yugoslavia.

**18** **Douglas Jardine,** the England cricket captain for the controversial 'Bodyline' series in 1932–33, died on this day in 1958, aged 57 (*see 17 January and 23 October*) ... **Henry Cooper** rocked the boxing world in 1963 by putting super-confident Cassius Clay on the canvas four seconds from the end of the fourth round of their non-title fight at Wembley. Clay's trainer Angelo Dundee later admitted that he made a small rip in Clay's glove into a bigger one during the interval so as to gain some extra time for his groggy fighter while a replacement glove was found.

A revived Clay renewed his attack in the next round and the referee stopped the fight with Cooper bleeding heavily from a cut over the eye ... Playing for Spain against Denmark in **1986 Emilio Butragueño** became the last man to score four goals in a match in the final stages of the World Cup.

## 19

The **first baseball match** took place at Elysian Fields, Hoboken (birthplace of Frank Sinatra!), New York, in **1846.** The New York Nine beat the sport's first organized club, the Knickerbocker Club, 23–1 ... One of the most successful batsmen in English cricket, **Walter Hammond,** was born in **1903.** He played for England 85 times between 1927 and 1947 and scored a then Test record 7249 runs. His 336 not out against New Zealand at Auckland in 1933 was also a Test record at the time. He scored 50,511 runs in first-class cricket ... England rugby international **Rory Underwood** was born in **1963.** England's most capped player, he made his debut against Ireland in 1984. A very talented and speedy winger, he is also England's top try-scorer, with 35 to his credit ... On this day in **1978 Ian Botham** completed a remarkable Test match against Pakistan at Lord's when he became the first man to score a century and take eight wickets in an innings (8–34).

## 20

At Wimbledon in **1949** American tennis player **Gussie Moran,** nicknamed 'Gorgeous Gussie', caused a sensation when she appeared wearing lace-trimmed knickers designed by Teddy Tinling (*see 23 June*). The knickers outraged the All-England Club so much that Tinling was not a welcome visitor at Wimbledon for 33 years ... South African-born Northants and

England Test cricketer **Allan Lamb** was born in **1954.** England vice-captain on the 1989–90 tour to the West Indies, he took over as skipper for the fourth and fifth Tests in Graham Gooch's absence ... Boxing history was made at the New York Polo Grounds in **1960** when **Floyd Patterson** knocked out Sweden's Ingemar Johansson in the fifth round to become the first man to regain the world heavyweight title and the first to beat the Swede. Patterson had lost his crown to Johansson a year earlier (*see 26 June*) ... **New Zealand beat France 29–9** at Auckland in **1987** to become the first winners of the Rugby Union World Cup.

# 21

Surrey and England cricketer **John Edrich** was born in **1937**. He scored 5138 runs in 77 Tests between 1963 and 1976. His 310 not out against New Zealand at Leeds in 1965 included a Test record 57 boundaries ... BBC television covered the **Wimbledon championships** for the first time in **1937** ... Tennis player **Maureen Connolly** died in **1969,** aged only 34 (*see 17 September*) ... Aston Villa and Wales striker **Dean Saunders** was born in **1964.** His started his career at Swansea, and then played for Cardiff on loan, Brighton, Oxford and Derby before moving to Liverpool for a British record £2.9 million in 1991. Saunders was not happy with the Merseyside club and after only one full season at Anfield he joined Aston Villa ... In **1970 Tony Jacklin** became the first Briton since Ted Ray in 1920 to win the US Open. While Jacklin was lifting the US Open golf title at Hazeltine, Minnesota, **Brazil** were winning the **1970** Jules Rimet Trophy, comfortably beating Italy 4–1 in Mexico. They were allowed to keep the trophy as this was their third win in the World Cup ... On this day in **1975** the **West Indies,** skippered by Clive Lloyd, beat Australia by 17 runs at Lord's to win the first cricket World Cup.

**22**

The **MCC and Hertfordshire** played the first match at the present-day Lord's Cricket Ground, St John's Wood, London, in **1814;** Yorkshireman Thomas Lord had previously opened grounds on the site of Dorset Square and at North Bank, St John's Wood ... **Joe Louis** became world heavyweight champion in **1937** by knocking out defending champion James J. Braddock in the eighth round at Comiskey Park, Chicago. The 'Brown Bomber' went on to make a record 25 defences before retiring in 1949. An attempt to regain the title the following year resulted in defeat by Ezzard Charles (*see 1 March*) ... Fast bowler **Michael Holding** set a NatWest Trophy record when he took 8 wickets for 21 runs for Derbyshire against Sussex at Hove in **1988 ... Chris Eubank** beat Michael Watson on points to retain his WBO middleweight title in 1991. It was the first boxing match at London's Earl's Court since Joe Bugner and Joe Frazier did battle in 1973.

**23**

**Teddy Tinling,** the man who brought a new meaning to tennis clothing, was born in **1910.** His designs for women players were eyecatching and revolutionary; the frilly lace knickers he devised for 'Gorgeous Gussie' Moran caused a stir at Wimbledon in 1949 (*see 20 June*). Tinling died in 1990 aged 79; at his request the theme tune to the TV show *Neighbours* was played at his memorial service! ... One of the all-time great England cricketers, **Sir Len Hutton,** was born in **1916.** A Yorkshireman through-and-through, he was the first professional captain of the England Test side. His innings of 364 against Australia at the Oval in 1938 stood as a Test record for nearly 20 years. He scored 6971 runs for England in 79 appearances between 1937 and 1955. He retired in 1960 with a total of 40,140 runs in first-class cricket to his credit. Sir Leonard died in 1990, aged 74 ... In **1973 Patricia's Hope** became only the second dog after Mick the Miller, in 1929 and 1930, to win the Greyhound Derby a second time.

## 24

Boxer **Jack Dempsey** was born in **1895** at Manassa, Colorado. Known as the 'Manassa Mauler', he won the heavyweight world title in 1919 by beating Jess Willard, the 17-stone (108 kg) cowboy from Kansas. He lost it on points to Gene Tunney in 1926 and in the following year 'was robbed of the title' in the infamous 'Battle of the Long Count' (*see 22 September*) ... The first great motor-racing world champion, **Juan Manuel Fangio** of Argentina, was born in **1911.** He won the title a record five times between 1951 and 1957. He won 24 world championship races, a record which stood until surpassed by the late Jim Clark in 1968. Fangio drove for all of the great manufacturers of the 1950s, winning world titles for Alfa Romeo, Maserati, Mercedes and Ferrari ... **BBC television covered a Test match for the first time in 1938** when they screened part of the second Test against Australia from Lord's. The highlight of the match was Walter Hammond's 240 in England's first innings.

# JUNE

**25**

In **1932** India made their Test cricket debut against England at Lord's. England, captained by Douglas Jardine, won by 158 runs ... **Joe Louis** made the 25th and last defence of his world heavyweight crown, against 'Jersey' Joe Walcott at the Yankee Stadium, New York, in **1948**. Louis won with an 11th-round knockout. Eight months later, he announced his retirement (*see 1 March*) ... At Wimbledon in **1969** Americans **Pancho Gonzales and Charlie Pasarell** engaged in the longest men's singles match on record. The 112 games took 5 hours and 12 minutes to complete. Gonzales came back from 22–24, 1–6 down to take the next three sets, 16–14, 6–3, 11–9, and the match.

**26**

The **first recorded women's cricket match** was played at Gosden Common, Surrey, in **1745** ... The **first motor-racing grand prix,** the French Grand Prix, was run at Le Mans in **1906.** The Romanian Ferenc Szisz drove a Renault to victory at an average speed of 63 mph (101 km/hr) ... The highest scoring match in the final stages of the **World Cup** occurred in the quarter-finals of the **1954** competition at Lausanne. The host nation, Switzerland, were beaten by neighbours Austria 7–5. Nine of the 12 goals were scored in a 23-minute spell in the first half ... At the Yankee Stadium, New York, in **1959 Ingemar Johansson** stopped Floyd Patterson in the third round of their contest to become the heavyweight champion of the world and the first non-American since Italy's Primo Carnera 25 years earlier to win the title. In the 1952 Olympic heavyweight final Johansson had been disqualified in the second round for 'not giving his best' and as a consequence had not been presented with his silver medal. The IOC rescinded their decision and gave him the medal in 1982 (*see 20 June*) ... The most successful American cyclist, **Greg LeMond,** was born in **1960.** Three times winner of the Tour de France, in 1986, 1989 and 1990, two of his wins came after he nearly lost his life in a freak shooting accident (*see 26 July*) ... In **1986** a record 39,813 people turned up to watch a single day's play at **Wimbledon**.

**27** Canada's **George Dixon** beat Nunc Wallace with an 18th round knockout in **1890** at the Pelican Club, London, to win the world bantamweight boxing title. It was the first world title fight under Queensberry Rules to be held in England ... **Muhammad Ali** announced his retirement from the boxing ring in **1979** after 59 professional fights dating back to 1960 (*see 29 October*). The announcement came nine months after he regained the world heavyweight title for the second time with a points win over Leon Spinks at New Orleans. However, Ali was tempted out of retirement a year later and in October 1980 unsuccessfully challenged Larry Holmes for the title.

**28** In **1930 Mick the Miller** won his second successive Greyhound Derby to become the first dog to win the race twice (*see 23 June*). ... At the small Brazilian mining town of Belo Horizonte in **1950** the **United States** brought off the biggest shock in the history of the World Cup by defeating joint tournament favourites England 1–0 in a group match. The England team contained some of the biggest names in the game: Billy Wright, Stan Mortensen, Bert Williams, Tom Finney and Wilf Mannion. The US team was made up of part-timers moulded together by

Scotsman Bill Jeffrey. Haiti-born Joseph 'Larry' Gaetjens scored the only goal, which came in the 37th minute. The result was flashed around the world but most newspapers thought the agencies had made a mistake and that the score line should have read 10–1 to England. How wrong they were! Gaetjens, the goalscoring hero, disappeared mysteriously during troubled times in his home country in 1970 ... FIFA announced the **first change in soccer's offside law** for 65 years in **1990** when they ruled that players *level* with defenders would, in future, be *on* side.

**29** The **Headingley** ground in Leeds was used for Test cricket for the first time in **1899** when England and Australia fought out a low-scoring draw ... **Susan Brown,** who made history in 1981 as the first woman to compete in the Boat Race, as cox, was born in **1958** ... The heaviest-ever world boxing champion, **Primo Carnera,** died in **1967** at the age of 60 (*see 26 October*).

**30** **England beat Australia 17–1** in Sydney in **1951** to record the biggest win in a football international, although the Football Association do not list the match as a full international ... The former world heavyweight boxing champion **Mike Tyson** was born in **1966.** He was only 20 years and 144 days old when he beat Trevor Berbick for the WBC version of the world championship in 1986, making him the youngest ever holder of the title. He went on to become the undisputed champion of the world, beating Tony Tucker in the following year. The seemingly invincible Tyson was knocked out in the 10th round of his bout with James 'Buster' Douglas in Tokyo in 1990. Tyson also had problems out of the ring, the break-up of his marriage to Robin Givens being followed by imprisonment for rape ... At Newcastle in **1990** jockey **Willie Carson** became only the third man, after Gordon Richards in 1933 and Alec Russell in 1957, to ride six winners at one race meeting. The winners, and prices, were: Arousal, evens favourite; Soweto 5–2 fav; Al Maheb 9–2; Terminus 8–1; Tadwin 5–1; Hot Desert 4–7 fav. In the seventh race of the meeting Carson came home last on Parliament Piece ... **Duke McKenzie** became the first British-based boxer to win world titles at two different weights; when he beat Gaby Canizales for the WBO bantamweight title at Southwark in **1991,** he had previously held the IBF flyweight title, between October 1988 and June 1989.

# JULY

# JULY

**1** Olympic champion **Carl Lewis** was born in **1961.** At the 1984
Los Angeles Olympics he emulated the great Jesse Owens by
winning four track and field gold medals, in the 100 and 200 m
sprint races, the long jump and the 4 × 100 m relay. He won
two more gold medals four years later and in 1992 took his tally
to eight golds with victories in the 4 × 100 m relay and in the
long jump for the third successive Games . . . Sharing a birthday
with Lewis is one of Britain's top cyclists of the 1980s, **Malcolm
Elliott,** who was also born in **1961.** After a successful career in
Britain, he established himself as a leading rider in Europe. He
won the Milk Race in 1987 and the Tour of Britain in 1988 . . .
Rugby league international **Garry Schofield** was born in **1965.**
He was the second youngest person to play for Great Britain
when he made his debut in 1984 . . . **BBC 2** began transmissions
in colour in Britain in **1967** with nearly seven hours' coverage
of the Wimbledon lawn tennis championships . . . In **1977 Virginia Wade** beat Betty Stove to win the ladies' singles title at
Wimbledon in, appropriately, Her Majesty the Queen's Silver
Jubilee Year . . . **Steve Ovett** deprived Sebastian Coe of his
world mile record in **1979** when he set a new best mark of 3
minutes 48.8 seconds in Oslo.

**2** The **first recorded speedway race** took place at Portman
Road, Ipswich, in **1904** . . . On the same day in **1904** French
lawn tennis star **René Lacoste** was born. He won the Wimbledon singles title in 1925 and 1928 and was a member of the
successful French Davis Cup team, dubbed the 'Four Musketeers', that won the trophy six times in succession between
1927 and 1932 . . . **Helen Wills-Moody** beat Helen Jacobs

6–4, 6–0 in **1938** to win a record eighth Wimbledon singles title. Martina Navratilova has since beaten her record (*see 7 July*).

**3** **Bramall Lane,** Sheffield, became England's seventh Test cricket ground when it staged the third Test between England and Australia in **1902**. Australia's Clem Hill scored the only century on the ground, which was not used again for Test cricket.... The world heavyweight boxing title fight between Marvin Hart and Jack Root at Nevada in **1905** was the first to have a former champion for a referee, **James J. Jeffries**. The contest was to find his successor ... In **1920 'Big' Bill Tilden** beat Gerald Patterson of Australia to become the first American winner of the men's singles title at Wimbledon ... The most prolific wicket-taker in Test cricket, former New Zealand and Nottinghamshire captain **Sir Richard Hadlee,** was born in **1951**. He became the first man to take 400 wickets in Test cricket in 1990. He was knighted for his services to cricket in the same year ... Britain's **Barry Sheene** won the 500cc race at the **1977** Belgian Grand Prix at an average speed of 135·07 mph (217 km/hr), the fastest ever recorded at a world championship motor-cycle race.

**4** **Jack Dempsey** beat Jess Willard to become world heavyweight boxing champion on this day in **1919**. Willard retired in the third round after being knocked down no fewer than seven times during their bout at Toledo, Ohio. ... Two days after Helen Wills-Moody won her record eighth Wimbledon title in **1938**, another darling of the centre court, **Suzanne Lenglen** of

France, died of leukaemia at the age of 39. She won a total of 15 titles between 1919 and 1925, six of them at Wimbledon in the ladies' singles ... Martina Navratilova's doubles partner, **Pam Shriver,** was born in **1962.** With Navratilova she won five Wimbledon titles and 21 Grand Slam doubles titles ... **Ann Jones** became Wimbledon champion in **1969** when she beat Billie-Jean King 3–6, 6–3, 6–2 in the final. The 30-year-old Briton had been unsuccessful in her 13 previous attempts, including a final against King two years earlier (*see 17 October*) ... In **1984 Alvin Kallicharan** set a Gillette/NatWest Cup record with an innings of 204 for Warwickshire against Oxford-shire.

**5**

**Dwight F. Davis,** the man who gave the Davis Cup to tennis, was born in **1879** ... Former England spin bowler **Tony Lock** was born on this day in **1929.** He took 174 wickets in 49 Tests between 1952 and 1968. He was a member of the successful Surrey county side in the 1950s ... There have been some notable achievements at Wimbledon on 5 July in years gone by: In **1919 Suzanne Lenglen** of France became the first non-English speaking ladies' champion; it was the first of five consecutive titles for Lenglen. In **1952 'Little Mo',** Maureen Connolly, won the ladies title at the age of 17, beating Louise Brough. **Arthur Ashe** became the first black men's champion in **1975** when he beat Jimmy Connors. In **1980 Bjorn Borg** won his fifth consecutive title, beating John McEnroe in a four-hour five-set cliffhanger rated as one of the best Wimbledon finals of all time.

**6** The best-known name in pre-war British motor racing, the **Brooklands** circuit, was opened in **1907.** The world's first purpose built race track came into being as a result of a ban on racing on Britain's roads ... On the same day in **1907, Tom Reece** completed the highest-ever billiards break with a staggering 499,135. The break, which had started on 3 June, was in the days of the now-outlawed 'craddle cannon' whereby a player could push the two object balls around the table all day by making a cannon each time. It must have been gripping stuff to watch! ... Northern Ireland track and field star **Mary Peters** was born in **1939.** She was the last-gasp winner of the pentathlon gold medal at the 1972 Munich Olympics, pipping her great rival Heidi Rosendahl of Germany by 10 points (*see 3 September*) ... And back to Wimbledon – on this day in **1957 Althea Gibson** of the United States became the first black Wimbledon champion when she beat Darlene Hard in straight sets to take the ladies' singles title.

**7** At The Oval in **1868 Edwin Pooley** of Surrey became the first wicketkeeper to dismiss 12 batsmen in one match, against Sussex ... Golfer **Tony Jacklin** was born in **1944.** When he won the British Open at Lytham in 1969 he became the first British winner for 18 years. Twelve months later he became the first British winner of the US Open for 50 years. He went on to skipper the European Ryder Cup side, guiding them to victory at The Belfry in 1985, the first by Britain or Europe since 1957, and two years later to an historic first-ever win on US soil ... American **Mark Hayes** became the first man to record a round of 63 in the British Open, in **1977** at Turnberry ... At Wimbledon in **1985** the unseeded **Boris Becker** became the youngest men's singles champion, aged only 17 ... **Martina Navratilova** beat Zina Garrison in just 75 minutes to win her record ninth Wimbledon singles title in **1990** ... As Martina was winning her ninth title, **Peter Shilton** was ending his international career. He played a record 125th and last time for England in the third place play-off match against Italy at Bari in the **1990** World Cup ... During the Torras Monte Carlo Open in **1990, Ian Woosnam** equalled David Llewellyn's European PGA Tour record by shooting a four-round total 258 (*see 3 April*).

**8**  Pugilist **Tom Cribb** was born in **1781.** Coincidentally, the **last bare-knuckle world heavyweight boxing contest** took place on Cribb's birthday in **1889,** when John L. Sullivan beat Jake Kilrain over 75 rounds at Richburg, Mississippi ... In **1961 Angela Mortimer** beat Christine Truman in the first all-British ladies' singles final at Wimbledon since 1914 ... Starting stalls were used for the first time in Britain in **1965,** in the Chesterfield Stakes at Newmarket ... **Ferrari** won its 100th formula one race at the Paul Ricard circuit in France in **1990.** The famous red marque, driven by Frenchman Alain Prost, took the chequered flag in the French Grand Prix.

**9**  The **first Wimbledon Lawn Tennis Championship** was held in **1877.** The only title, the men's singles, was won by Spencer Gore, who beat his fellow Briton W.C. Marshall 6–1, 6–2, 6–4 ... On this day in **1922** 18-year-old **Johnny Weissmuller** became the first swimmer to cover 100 metres in under one minute when he set a new world record time of 58·6 seconds. (*see 2 June*) ... In **1954** Australia's **Peter Thomson** won the first of his five British Open titles, and the first of three in successive years ... **Ian Botham** scored 200 runs in 219 balls against India at The Oval in **1982,** the fastest Test double-century in terms of balls delivered.

## 10

The former Leeds United and England soccer manager **Don Revie** was born in **1927.** He transformed Leeds from a struggling second division side into one of the best teams in Europe in the 1960s. He guided them to two Championships, one FA Cup win, a League Cup win and glory in Europe. Revie quit the England manager's job in 1977 after a less successful time, and took his talents to the Gulf ... Tennis played **Arthur Ashe** was born in **1943.** The first black men's Wimbledon champion in 1975 he was responsible for the formation of the Association of Tennis Professionals (ATP). He contracted the AIDS virus following a blood transfusion during open-heart surgery and died in 1993 of an AIDS-related disease ... Britain's most successful female tennis player of the 1970s, **Virginia Wade,** was born in **1945.** She won the coveted Wimbledon title in 1977 (*see 1 July*) ... Indian cricketer **Sunil Gavaskar** was born in **1949.** He was the first man to score 10,000 Test runs. His total of 10,122 runs was achieved in 125 Tests ... In **1951** Midlander **Randolph Turpin** became the first Briton since Bob Fitz-simmons last century to win the world middleweight crown. It was champion 'Sugar' Ray Robinson's first defence of the title. At the end of 15 gruelling rounds with the hard-punching Turpin he had lost his title and gained a badly cut eye requiring 14 stitches (*see 12 September*) ... In **1970 David Broome,** on Beethoven, became the first British male to win the world showjumping championship ... Snooker player **Joe Davis** died in **1978** (*see 15 April*) ... Former Celtic Soccer player **Maurice Johnston** was transferred to Glasgow Rangers, from French club Nantes, for £1·5 million in **1989.** He was the first big-name Roman Catholic player to be signed by the club, which had a tradition of fielding only Protestants.

**11**

**Old Trafford,** Manchester, became the second British Test cricket ground after the Kennington Oval when it hosted the first Test between England and Australia in **1884.** England were dismissed for just 95 runs in their first innings. The match was drawn ... **Leon Spinks,** one half of the only pair of brothers to win the world heavyweight boxing crown (*see 13 July*), was born in **1953.** Spinks won the title by beating Muhammad Ali in 1978, but he lost it again to Ali seven months later and in 1981 failed to regain it from Larry Holmes. Spinks and his brother Michael both won gold medals at the 1976 Montreal Olympics.

**12**

In **1930** Australia's **Don Bradman** scored 309 runs in a single day's play against England in the third Test at Headingley, Leeds; no one has scored more runs in a day in a Test match. Bradman's score of 334 runs in Australia's innings total of 556 was a new Test record. The match was drawn ... The most economical bowling spell in first-class cricket was had by Yorkshire bowler **Hedley Verity** in **1932.** He took 10 Nottinghamshire wickets for only 10 runs at Headingley ... **Gareth**

**Edwards**, one of the stars of the successful Welsh rugby side of the 1960s and 1970s, was born in **1947**. He played for his country 53 times between 1967 and 1978 and did not miss a game for Wales from the start to the end of his international career. He is the second most-capped Welshman, after J. P. R. Williams, and has a Welsh record 20 tries to his credit. Edwards played for the British Lions ten times ... In **1969 Tony Jacklin** became the first home winner of the British Open since Max Faulkner in 1951. A fine opening round of 68 set up his victory at Lytham St Annes. He ended up beating the left-handed New Zealander Bob Charles by two strokes with a four round total of 280 ... In **1992 Graham Gooch** became the most successful batsman in Sunday League cricket when he surpassed Denis Amiss' record of 7040 runs.

**13** Italian racing driver **Alberto Ascari** was born in **1918**. The first man to win successive world titles, in 1952 and 1953, he lost his life while testing a new Ferrari at Monza in 1955. Three days earlier Ascari had survived a dramatic crash into the harbour at Monte Carlo ... The **first World Cup soccer match** was contested when France met Mexico at the Pocitos Stadium, Montevideo, on this day in **1930**. A crowd of about one thousand witnessed the historic match, which France won 4–1. The first World Cup goal was scored by France's inside-left, Lucien Laurent, after 19 minutes ... **Michael Spinks,** brother of Leon (*see 11 July*) was born in **1956**. He defeated Eddie Mustafa Muhammad for the WBA light-heavyweight title in 1981. He switched to heavyweight after ten successful defences and became the first man to inflict a defeat on Larry

Holmes, in 1985, to take the IBF heavyweight title. He was the first man to win the light-heavyweight crown and then take the heavyweight title. He was dethroned by Mike Tyson, who knocked him out in the first round of their title fight in 1988 ... Snooker player **Neal Foulds** was born in **1963.** Number three in the world rankings in 1987, his form declined dramatically after suffering personal problems. He regained his form in the 1990s and is again a threat to the top players.

**14**

**Andrew Awford** was born on this day in **1972.** The name is not well known in the sporting world, but on 10 October 1987 Andrew made soccer history as the youngest person to play in the FA Cup. He was only 15 years and 88 days old when he appeared for Worcester City against Borehamwood in a qualifying round tie. ... The **Welsh Rugby Union team** suffered the biggest defeat in its history in **1991** when it was trounced 71–8 by New South Wales. It was the first time since 1881 that a Welsh side had conceded 13 tries in a match. Further misery was in store for the Welsh tourists: seven days after the New South Wales defeat, they were soundly beaten 63–6 by Australia in the Brisbane Test match.

**15**

Cricketing history was made at Colchester, Essex, in **1938** when **Arthur Fagg** scored an unbeaten 202 not out in Kent's second innings against Essex. He had already made 244 in the first innings and is the only man to score double centuries in both innings of a first-class match ... At Royal Birkdale in **1983** **Dennis Durnian** established a record score for nine holes in the British Open when he shot a 28 in the second round ...

**Laurie Cunningham,** the second black footballer to play for England after Viv Anderson, was killed in a car crash near Madrid in **1989,** aged 33. Cunningham made his name with Leyton Orient and West Bromwich before moving to top Spanish club Real Madrid.

# 16

On this day in **1895 Archie MacLaren** of Lancashire completed the highest innings in first-class cricket in Britain and, at the time, in the world. MacLaren took seven hours and 50 minutes to complete his record-breaking innings of 424, against Somerset at Taunton. Worcestershire's Graeme Hick is the only other batsman to score 400 runs in England. His unbeaten 405 was scored on the same ground, Taunton, in 1988 . . . Australian tennis player **Margaret Court** was born in **1942.** She won more Grand Slam titles, 66, than any other player. Her total includes 26 singles titles. She won the Wimbledon singles title in 1963, 1965 (both under her maiden name, Smith) and 1970 . . . The final match in the **1950** World Cup between **Brazil and Uruguay** at the Maracana Stadium, Rio de Janeiro, was watched by 199,854 people, although the paying attendance was *only* 172,772 . . . The **British Lions** suffered their biggest defeat ever in **1983** when beaten 38–6 by the All Blacks in Auckland . . . **Brazil,** the one-time giants of world soccer, beat Uruguay 1–0 in the final of the **1989** South American Championship. Remarkably, it was their first major title since the 1970 World Cup.

**17** The former Derbyshire and England wicketkeeper **Bob Taylor** was born in **1941.** He kept wicket 57 times for England and dismissed 174 batsmen. His total of 1649 dismissals is a record in first-class cricket. Against India in 1980 he equalled the Test record with seven dismissals (all caught) in one innings ... **Sebastian Coe** first broke the mile world record at Oslo in **1979,** knocking four-tenths of a second off John Walker's four-year-old record to set a new time of 3 minutes 48·95 seconds. Exactly four years earlier, on 17 July **1975,** Coe had first run a sub-four minute mile.

**18** One of the most celebrated of all British sportsmen, **William Gilbert 'W.G.' Grace,** was born in **1848.** Unquestionably one of cricket's great characters, 'The Doctor'—Grace qualified as a GP—was an outstanding all-rounder; he scored 54,896 runs, and took 2876 first-class wickets and 871 catches. In 1876 he became the first man to score 300 runs in an innings; for good measure, he performed this feat twice in a week! He spent most of his career with his home county, Gloucestershire. Also a keen lawn bowler, playing for England at international level, he formed the English Bowling Association in 1903 and was its president until 1905. He retired from first-class cricket at the age of 60, in 1908, and died in 1915 (*see 23 October*) ... Athlete **David Hemery** was born in **1948.** Hemery's brilliant world record run in the 400 metres hurdles at the 1968 Mexico Olympics won him the gold medal—it also resulted in commentator David Coleman nearly losing his voice with excitement! ... Australian fast bowler **Dennis Lillee** was born in **1949.** His aggregate of 355 wickets in 70 Test matches was a record until surpassed by Ian Botham ... **'Jersey' Joe Walcott** knocked out Ezzard Charles in **1951** to become the oldest world heavyweight boxing champion at 37 years and 168 days ... The most successful British golfer of modern times, **Nick Faldo,** was born in **1957.** Faldo was the first Briton since Henry Cotton to win the British Open three times, in 1987, 1990 and 1992. He also emulated the great Jack Nicklaus in winning the US Masters in successive years, in 1989 and 1990.

## 19

**Maurice Garin** of France won the inaugural Tour de France cycle race in **1903.** ... The brilliant but temperamental Romanian tennis player **Ilie Nastase** was born in **1946.** He won the French and US Championships but was twice beaten in the singles final at Wimbledon: by Stan Smith in 1972 and Bjorn Borg in 1976. ... At the Bogside race course in **1957 Alec Russell** became only the second man, after Gordon Richards in 1933, to ride all six winners at one meeting. Russell's six winners were: Double Up 2–5 favourite, Cligarry 2–1 fav, Wage Claim 100–8, Courtlier 8–1, Newton 8–13 fav, and Roselime 11–8 fav.

## 20

The idea of a **Football Association Challenge Cup** competition was first mooted by Charles Alcock, secretary of the FA, at a meeting in **1871** ... Fourteen years to the day after that first meeting, in **1885,** the **Football Association** legalized professionalism. Many clubs, notably Preston North End, admitted they had been paying their players ... The former Liverpool and England striker **Roger Hunt** was born in **1938.** Liverpool's all-time record goalscorer with 245 league goals until surpassed by Ian Rush in 1992, he appeared for England in the 1966 World Cup final and in 34 games for England scored 18 goals ... Top table tennis player **Desmond Douglas** was born in **1955.** He won a record 25 English national titles between 1976 and 1990 ... In **1986 Frank Bruno** challenged Tim Witherspoon for the world heavyweight crown. Despite a brave effort, Bruno was knocked out in the eleventh round. In his second attempt to win the title, almost three years later, Bruno was stopped in the fifth round by Mike Tyson ... **Australia beat Papua New Guinea 70–8** at Wagga Wagga in **1988** to register the biggest win in a rugby league international.

**21**

**Lord's cricket ground** hosted its first Test Match in **1884** when it staged the second Test between England and Australia. England won by an innings and five runs ... Darts player **John Lowe** was born in **1945.** The Derbyshire-born player once won £102,000 for a nine-dart finish (*see 13 October*). Lowe has won all the sport's top prizes, including the world title. In 1993 he showed he had lost none of his sparkle, winning the Embassy championship to add to his world titles in 1979 and 1987 ... The Tottenham Hotspur inside-forward **John White** was tragically killed on this day in **1964,** struck by lightning while sheltering from a storm during a round of golf on the links at Crews Hill, Enfield ... In **1968 Arnold Palmer** became the first man to win $1 million on the US golf Tour when he tied for second place in the US PGA Championship at Pecan Valley, Texas ... **David Platt** completed his £5.5 million move from Aston Villa to Bari in **1991** to become the most expensive British footballer.

**22** The former BBC television *Match of the Day* presenter **Jimmy Hill** was born in **1928.** Hill made his name as a player with Fulham; later he would become the club's chairman. He managed Coventry City between 1961 and 1967, trebling the gates and guiding the club into the first division for the first time in its history. However, shortly before the club's debut game in the first division, he quit to take a top job with the new London Weekend Television company. Then he moved to the BBC. Hill has contributed a great deal to the game and has always sought a better deal for players ... **Lasse Viren,** the top Finnish long-distance runner, was born in **1949.** He won gold in the 5000 and 10,000 metres at the 1972 and 1976 Olympics to become the only man to win both races at consecutive Games.

**23** In **1949 Brian Close** of Yorkshire made his debut for England against New Zealand at Old Trafford to become England's youngest Test cricketer, he was aged 18 years and 149 days at the time ... Another England Test cricketer, **Graham Gooch,** was born in **1953.** He made his Test debut in 1975, but was banned from Test cricket after leading the England rebels against South Africa in 1982. He returned to captain the side to a memorable victory over the West Indies in the Caribbean in 1990. Gooch capped this auspicious start to the year with a record-breaking performance against India (*see 30 July*) ... British cyclist **Tommy Simpson** died of exhaustion on Mount Ventoux during the **1967** Tour de France. Simpson, the first Englishman to wear the prized yellow jersey in the Tour de France, collapsed on the gruelling 13th Marseilles–Avignon stage, in intense heat. The last words of the 29-year-old former world road-race champion were 'Put me back on my bike'. As a token of respect, the other riders allowed another Briton, Barry Hoban, to ride through and take the next stage the following day ... Former Pakistan cricketer **Jahangir Khan** died in **1988** at the age of 78. He entered the annals of cricket lore because at Lord's in 1932 one of his deliveries hit a sparrow in flight and killed it. The sparrow, stuffed and mounted on a cricket ball, is now displayed in the Lord's museum ... **Greg LeMond** won the Tour de France for the second time in **1989,** beating Laurent Fignon by a mere eight seconds ... Also in **1989,** Britain's **Mike Russell** became the youngest world professional billiards champion at the age of 20 years and 49 days. He defeated Peter Gilchrist for the title at Leura, Australia.

**24** **Matthew Webb,** the first man to swim the English Channel (*see 25 August*), died in **1883,** aged 35, while attempting to swim the rapids above Niagara Falls. ... The **first greyhound meeting** with a mechanical hare took place at Belle Vue, Manchester, in **1926**.

**25** In **1914 W. G. Grace** scored 69 not out for Eltham against Grove Park in his last cricket match. He was 66 at the time (*see 18 July*) ... The NFL's all-time top rusher, **Walter Payton**, was born in **1954.** Playing for the Chicago Bears, Payton rushed for a career record 16,726 yards between 1975 and 1987 and scored 109 touchdowns, only 17 short of Jim Brown's record ... In **1965** the former world light-heavyweight boxing champion **Freddie Mills** was found shot dead in his car in Soho, London. A verdict of suicide was recorded but the circumstances in which he died has cast doubt in some minds as to the accuracy of this judgement (*see 26 July*) . . . A record **172 nations** were represented at the XXVth Olympics which opened in Barcelona in **1992**. The opening ceremony was watched on TV by an estimated 3·5 billion people worldwide. The Spanish hosts defied their critics and staged one of the most successful Games ever.

## 26

**John McGregor** founded the first Canoe Club at Richmond, Surrey, on this day in **1866** . . . **Freddie Mills** beat Gus Lesnevich on points over 15 rounds at London's White City in **1948** to capture the world light-heavyweight title. He had lost to Lesnevich in his first attempt to take the title two years earlier. A gutsy but unexceptional fighter, Mills retired from the ring after losing his title to American Joey Maxim, who knocked him out in the 10th round of their contest, Mills' first defence, in January 1950 (*see 25 July*) . . . In **1966 Tony Brown** of Gloucestershire equalled Mickey Stewart's first-class cricket record of an outfielder taking seven catches in an innings, against Nottinghamshire at Trent Bridge . . . **Muhammad Ali** won his first title since returning to boxing after his enforced lay-off, beating Jimmy Ellis for the North American heavyweight title in **1971** (*see 29 April*) . . . In **1987 Stephen Roche** became the first Irishman to win the Tour de France cycle race and only the second winner from outside continental Europe; the first was America's Greg LeMond in 1986.

**27** Australian cricket captain **Allan Border** was born in 1955. The world's most capped cricketer, he surpassed Sunil Gavaskar's Test record of 10,122 runs in 1993. He has also held more catches than any other outfielder in Test cricket. . . . **Christopher Dean,** one half of the successful British ice-dance partnership, was born in 1958. The former Nottingham policeman teamed up with Jayne Torvill to win the World championship four times in a row (1981–84) and the Olympic title in 1984. Their reign raised standards in the sport to an unprecedented level, and the judges would frequently be unanimous in awarding the perfect mark 6, for their sizzling, inventive routines . . . **Steve Cram** set the mile world record at 3 minutes 46·32 seconds at Oslo in 1985, a time still standing as a record in August 1993 . . . **Graham Gooch** became the first Englishman since John Edrich to score a Test triple century when he scored 333 in the first innings against India at Lord's in 1990 (*see 30 July*) . . . In Australia's 40–15 win over England at Sydney in 1991 **David Campese** became the first man to score 40 tries in international rugby union. In the same match, **Michael Lynagh** became the first to score 600 points at international level . . . **Alan Shearer** was transferred from Southampton to Blackburn Rovers in 1992 for a record fee of £3·6 million as part of their new manager, Kenny Dalglish's plan to bring honours to the Lancashire club.

**28** **Sir Garfield Sobers,** one of the finest and most respected cricketers of all-time, was born in 1936. A great all-rounder, he took 235 wickets and scored a then-record 8032 runs in 93 Test matches. In 1958 he surpassed Len Hutton's Test record at Kingston, Jamaica, by one run when he scored an unbeaten 365 against Pakistan. Ten years later, playing for Nottinghamshire against Glamorgan at Swansea, he hit Malcolm Nash for 36 runs in one over, a record in first-class cricket . . . **Laura Davies** became the first British winner of the US Women's Open golf championship in **1987** beating JoAnne Carner and Ayoko Okamoto in a play-off at Plainfield, New Jersey . . . **Dennis Andries** became the first British boxer to regain a world title *twice* when in **1990** he beat Jeff Harding in a world light-heavyweight title fight at Melbourne.

## 29

The most famous bowls match in history took place on this day in **1588**—or so legend has it. **Sir Francis Drake** was playing bowls on Plymouth Hoe when he received news that the Spanish Armada was off the coast of Cornwall . . . The first **Olympic Games** since 1936 opened at Wembley Stadium, London, in **1948** . . . The 1986 World professional snooker champion **Joe Johnson** was born in **1952** . . . In **1989** the Cuban high-jumper **Javier Sotomayor** became the first man to clear eight feet (2.44 m), at San Juan, Puerto Rico.

## 30

The first world title fight under Queensberry rules took place at Staten Island, New York, in **1884, Jack 'Nonpareil' Dempsey** beating George Fulljames by a knockout in the 22nd round to win the world middleweight title . . . The first **soccer World Cup** came to a close in **1930** with the host nation, Uruguay, beating neighbours Argentina 4–2 in the Centenary Stadium, Montevideo . . . Decathlete **Daley Thompson** was born in **1958.** Winner of the Olympic gold medal in 1980 and 1984, he also won Commonwealth, European and World titles . . . The

**1966** World Cup final at Wembley gave **England,** the pioneers of football, their first overall victory in the competition. After conceding an early goal to West Germany, England pulled back to lead 2–1 with only seconds of the match remaining but Weber scored a last-gasp equalizer. The most controversial goal in World Cup history came in extra time, Geoff Hurst turning and cannoning the ball against the underside of the crossbar. The ball bounced down and over the line—or did it? Nevertheless, a goal was awarded, putting England ahead 3–2. Geoff Hurst completed his hat-track in the last seconds of the game as fans ran on to the pitch, and Kenneth Wolstenholme uttered those immortal words: 'They think it's all over. It is now' ... In the second innings against India at Lord's in **1990, Graham Gooch** made 123 runs to add to his first innings of 333, a match aggregate of 456 runs and a record in Test cricket. The match was also the first in which a batsman had scored a triple century and a century. The total of 1603 runs the match yielded was the second highest ever scored in a Test in England.

**31**

The former England cricket captain **G. O. 'Gubby' Allen** was born in **1902.** He was three months short of his 46th birthday when he played in his 25th and last Test match in the West Indies in 1948. He died in 1989 aged 87 ... **Heather McKay**, the most successful female squash player in the history of the sport, was born in **1941.** Australian-born, she held the British Open title for 16 years, between 1962 and 1977. She also won the World Open title in 1976 and 1979 ... Australian tennis player **Evonne Goolagong** (later Cawley) was born in **1951.** She beat fellow Australian Margaret Court to win her first

Wimbledon title at the age of 20 in 1971. Almost a decade later, in 1980, she beat Chris Evert to win her second title ... The most remarkable bowling feat in the history of Test cricket was completed at Old Trafford in **1956** when **Jim Laker** took his 19th Australian wicket for 90 runs. He had taken 9 for 37 in the first innings and followed that by taking all 10 Australian wickets for 53 runs in the second innings. England won the Test, the fourth in the series, by an innings and 170 runs (*see 16 May*).

# AUGUST

**1** The oldest surviving sporting contest, the **Doggett's Coat and Badge,** for Thames scullers, was first held in **1716.** It was the idea of Irish comedian Thomas Doggett ... American tennis player **Jack Kramer** was born in **1921.** The Wimbledon champion in 1947, he also won successive US titles in 1946 and 1947. A pioneer of the professional game in the 1950s, he later found fame behind the microphone ... The XIth Olympics opened in Berlin in **1936. Hitler** used the Games as a propaganda vehicle to promote his idea of Aryan supremacy. The black American athlete Jesse Owens turned this notion on its head by winning four gold medals ... Six days after surprisingly losing to Steve Ovett in the 800 metres final at the Moscow Olympics in **1980 Sebastian Coe** turned the tables by beating Ovett into third place to win the 1500 metres gold medal; Jürgen Straub of East Germany took the silver ... **Australia** won the fourth Test at Old Trafford in **1989** to become the first Australian side to *regain* the Ashes *in* England since 1934; it was also Australia's 100th win over England.

**2** The former Northern Ireland soccer player **Sammy McIlroy** was born in **1954.** A member of the successful Manchester United team of the 1970s, he scored a goal on his debut for the club in the Manchester 'Derby' in 1971. He made over 400 appearances for United before moving to a struggling Stoke City and then returning to the top flight with Manchester City. He later played for Bury and then moved to Sweden. He won 88 Northern Ireland caps ... **Mike Tyson** beat the IBF champion Tony Tucker on points over 12 rounds at Las Vegas in **1987** to become the first universal world heavyweight champion since Leon Spinks in 1978 ... Snooker player Ronnie O'Sullivan's record run of 38 consecutive wins in ranking tournaments was ended in **1992** by **Sean Storey**.

**3** Argentine footballer **Osvaldo 'Ossie' Ardíles** was born in **1953.** He and fellow Argentine Ricky Villa caused a stir in the late 1970s when they joined Tottenham Hotspur and set a modern-day trend for future overseas players in the Football League. Both players made an immediate impact, and Ossie stayed in Britain after his playing days to go into management, taking charge of Swindon before moving to West Bromwich and in 1993 replacing Terry Venables at Spurs. He won a World Cup winners' medal with Argentina in 1978 ... Another footballer who caused a transfer sensation on this day in **1957** was Leeds United and Wales centre-half or centre-forward **John Charles,** who moved to the Italian club Juventus for £65,000. He enjoyed a successful spell in Italy and spent five seasons with Juventus. He briefly returned to Leeds in 1962, but went back to Italy to finish the season with Roma before finally coming home to his native Wales and finishing his career at Cardiff City.

**4** In **1945** American golfer **Byron Nelson** won the Canadian Open to notch up his 11th consecutive tournament victory. He finished fourth in his next tournament, the Memphis Open, but went on to win a further seven tournaments in the year to give him a record 18 'firsts' on the US Tour ... In **1957** the Argentine racing driver **Juan Manual Fangio** won the German Grand Prix at the Nürburgring to clinch his record-breaking fifth, and last, world title. The race was also the 24th and last grand prix win of his career, a record at the time. Unlike the other drivers, Fangio started the race with the fuel tank of his Maserati half full. He drove carefully until the halfway stage at which point he refuelled. He came out of the pits with a deficit of 45 seconds to make up. The 46-year-old proceeded to break the track record in lap after lap, eventually overhauling the race leaders to take the chequered flag ... In **1976 women played cricket at Lord's for the first time,** an England team beating Australia by eight wickets in a limited 60-overs match.

## 5

The former Liverpool, Tottenham and England goalkeeper **Ray Clemence** was born in **1948.** He started his career at Scunthorpe and went on to win all the top honours in British and European football. He played for England 61 times and vied with Peter Shilton for the No. 1 jersey. On retiring, Clemence joined the coaching team at White Hart Lane ... In **1970 Manchester United** became the first senior team in British football to win a competitive match by a penalty shoot-out. Their Watney Cup semi-final against Hull City stood at 1–1 after 90 minutes. The final score was 4–3 after penalties. United were beaten 4–1 by Derby County in the final ... Aberdeen's new **Pittodrie Stadium,** the first all-seater stadium in Britain, was inaugurated in **1978** by a friendly between the home side and Tottenham Hotspur ... In **1990 Tom Kite** won the Federal Express St Jude Classic at Memphis to become the first golfer to win $6 million on the US PGA Tour ... **Paul Parker** became Manchester United's second £2 million footballer in **1991,** signing from Queen's Park Rangers.

**6** In **1926** 19-year-old New Yorker **Gertrude Ederle** became the first woman to swim the English Channel. She made the crossing from Cap Gris-Nez to Deal in 14 hours 39 minutes, cutting some two hours off the record ... **Stirling Moss** enjoyed the 16th and last formula one win of his career at the Nürburgring in **1961** when he won the German Grand Prix in a Lotus-Climax. Four times runner-up in the world championship, he was the most successful English-born formula one driver until the advent of Nigel Mansell (*see 23 April*) ... In **1991** Ukrainian pole-vaulter **Sergey Bubka** cleared 20 feet (6·09 m) at Malmö in Sweden to set a new world record of 20 feet and one-quarter inch (6·17 m). It was the 13th time Bubka had set an outdoor world record ... On the same day in **1991**, and the day after Manchester United forked out £2 million for Paul Parker, Manchester City paid Wimbledon £2.3 million for **Keith Curle,** making him most expensive defender in the Football League.

**7** On this day in **1711 Queen Anne** attended the Ascot race meeting, thus earning it the prefix 'Royal'. The modern-day meeting, held every June, hosts some of the best-known races in the turf calendar, including the Gold Cup and the Royal Hunt Cup ... The **first British Grand Prix** was raced at Brooklands in **1926.** Known as the RAC Grand Prix, the race was won by Sénéchal and Wagner in a Delage at an average speed of 71·61 mph (115·22 km/hr) ... Australian cricketer **Greg Chappell** was born in **1948.** He played for his country 87 times, scored 7110 runs and took 122 catches. Against New Zealand at Wellington in 1973 he scored an aggregate 380 runs in the match, a Test record until surpassed by Graham Gooch in 1990 (*see 30*

*July*). He captained Australia 48 times ... Top flat-race jockey **Walter Swinburn** was born in **1961.** Two Derbys are among his many big-race wins, in 1981 on Shergar, and in 1986 on Shahrastani. His father, Walter senior, was also a jockey.

**8** The inaugural **Davis Cup** got under way on this day in **1900** at Boston, Massachusetts. The idea of a contest between international teams was put forward by US doubles champion and Harvard undergraduate Dwight Filley Davis, who donated a cup. The competition, known as 'The International Lawn Tennis Championship', would be held annually, with the winners having to accept a challenge for the trophy the following year. Since 1972 the Davis Cup has been played on a knockout basis. The first winners of the Cup were the United States, who beat Britain 3–0 over three days' play. Dwight Davis played in both singles and doubles ... The most successful British motor-racing driver to date, **Nigel Mansell,** was born in **1954.** He started his formula one career at Lotus and had his first win in the 1985 European Grand Prix. After twice coming close to taking the world title with the Williams team, he moved to Ferrari but returned to Williams in 1991. He was crowned world champion at the end of the 1992 season, which he had dominated. In 1993 he made his debut in Indy car racing in the United States.

**9** **Rod Laver,** the first man to achieve a Grand Slam in lawn Tennis twice (1962 and 1969), was born in Australia in **1938.** Laver won Wimbledon titles in 1961 and 1962 and in 1968 and 1969 ... British decathlete **Daley Thompson** set a new world record of 8847 points to retain his Olympic title at the **1984** Games in Los Angeles . . . One of soccer's most loved characters, **Joe Mercer,** died on this day in **1990,** aged 76. The former Everton and Arsenal wing-half, and also former Footballer of the Year, had spells managing Sheffield United and Aston Villa before joining Manchester City in 1965 and guiding the club to the League title in the 1967–68 season.

# 10

The **first long-distance car race,** which had started in Peking on 10 June, ended in Paris on this day in **1907.** The race was won by Prince Borghese of Italy driving an Itala . . . British swimmer **Anita Lonsbrough** was born in **1941.** She won the 200 metres breaststroke gold medal at the Rome Olympics in 1960. She later married cyclist Hugh Porter . . . Top rugby league player **Andy Gregory** was born in Wigan in **1941.** Only 5 feet 4 inches (1.62 m) tall, Gregory made his name with Widnes before eventually moving to his illustrious hometown team for a large fee. He has appeared in a record nine Challenge Cup finals and collected a winner's medal on a record seven occasions . . . Jockey **Sir Gordon Richards** announced his retirement in **1954** after 21,843 winning rides. His last race at Sandown on 10 July had ended with 'severe' injuries following a fall . . . On this day in **1984** spectators in the Los Angeles Coliseum witnessed one of the biggest controversies in recent Olympic history. Local favourite **Mary Decker** tripped over the leg of 'British' athlete Zola Budd during the final of the 3000 metres and tumbled out of the race. Many in the partisan crowd interpreted Decker's fall as a deliberate trip by Budd and booed her at the end of the race. Budd was disqualified at first, although she had not finished among the medal winners, and then reinstated in seventh place when film of the race revealed that Decker's 'aggressive tactics' had caused the incident (*see 26 May*).

## 11

**Les Ames** became the first wicketkeeper to score 100 centuries in a career in first-class cricket, at Canterbury in **1950.** His 131 set Kent on their way to a four-wicket victory over arch-rivals Middlesex on the last day of Canterbury Week ... A crowd of 33,000 attended a testimonial match for the former Manchester United manager **Sir Matt Busby** at Old Trafford in **1991**. The match, a 1–1 draw between United and a Republic of Ireland XI, yielded a staggering £250,000 for the man who turned United into one of the first truly great post-war English teams ... The giant-hitting **John Daly** came from nowhere to win the **1991** US PGA title at the Crooked Stick course in Indiana. A Tour 'rookie', and ninth reserve for the tournament, he came into the event as the last entrant and went on to provide one of the biggest upsets in recent years, outdriving his rivals to win the title by three strokes from Bruce Lietzke.

## 12

In **1936 Marjorie Gestring** of the United States became the youngest winner of an individual Olympic gold medal when she won the springboard diving title at the Berlin Games; she was only 13 years and 286 days old at the time ... **Bert Sutcliffe** scored 100 not out in the second innings of New Zealand's game against Essex at Southend in **1949** to become the first member of a New Zealand touring side to score two centuries in a match in England; he scored 243 in the first innings, the highest made by a New Zealand tourist in England. He also became the first New Zealander to score 2000 runs in a season ... American long-jumper **Ralph Boston** set a new world record in **1960** with a leap of 8·21 metres (26 feet 11¼), breaking the record of 8·13 (26 feet 8¼ inches) set by Jesse Owens at Ann Arbor, Michigan, in 1935 (*see 25 May*) ... **Pete Sampras,** the youngest winner of the men's singles at the US Lawn Tennis Championships, was born in **1971.** He was only 19 years and 28 days old when he won the title in 1990 (*see 9 September*). He won his first Wimbledon singles title in 1993.

**13**

Tennis player **Jean Borotra**, a member of the successful French Davis Cup team of the 1920s, dubbed the 'Four Musketeers', was born in **1898.** Borotra, nicknamed the 'Bounding Basque,' was the first Frenchman to win the men's singles at Wimbledon in 1924 ... One of the finest early post-war American golfers, **Ben Hogan,** was born in **1912.** He won nine Majors, including the US Open four times. His win in the 1950 Open came only a year after an horrific car crash which nearly claimed his life. In 1953 he became the first man to win three majors in one year. Had the US PGA Championship not clashed with the British Open, which he won, Hogan would probably have won that as well to complete a remarkable grand slam ... In **1948 Boris Stankovic** of Yugoslavia went into the record books as the first soccer player to be sent off in a match at Wembley. He received his marching orders in the final of the Olympic soccer tournament. Sweden won the match 3–2 ... Britain's costliest footballer, **Alan Shearer,** was born in **1970.** Newcastle-born Shearer started his senior career on the south coast, with Southampton, before a £3·6 million move to Blackburn Rovers in 1992. His goal-scoring talents put Rovers at the top of the Premier League until injury cut short his season and with it Blackburn's hopes of the title.

**14**

Billiards and snooker player **Fred Davis** was born in **1913.** The younger brother of the famous Joe Davis, Fred come into his own after Joe's retirement. He was the world professional snooker champion three times and held the Professional Match-Play title (the world title in all but name) for five years, between 1952 and 1956. He captured his first world billiards title in 1980, at the age of 67 . . . Australian batsman **Donald Bradman** was given a standing ovation as he went to the crease for his last innings in Test cricket at The Oval in **1948**. Needing only four runs for a career Test match average of 100, he was dismissed second ball by Eric Hollies. It is said Bradman had tears in his eyes as he faced the delivery from Hollies and did not see the ball properly. His career ended with a Test average of 99·94. He was knighted in 1949, the year of his retirement from the game (*see 27 August*).

**15**

Off-spinner **Pat Pocock** had one of the most prolific spells in first-class cricket while playing for Surrey against Sussex at Eastbourne in **1972.** He took five wickets in six balls, six wickets in nine balls and seven in eleven balls . . . **Sebastian Coe** broke his third world record in six weeks at Zurich in **1979** when he set a new best for the 1500 metres; the other records broken in this extraordinary phase were for the 800 metres and the mile.

**16** Bare-knuckle fighter **Jack Broughton,** known as the 'Father of Boxing', published the first set of boxing rules on this day in **1743.** He devised the rules in response to the death of an opponent, Yorkshireman George Stevenson, who had died of injuries suffered in a bout with Broughton two years earlier. Broughton's rules—which outlawed head-butting, gouging, kicking and similar street-fighting techniques—remained in force until superseded by the London Prize Rules one hundred years later (*see 24 April*) ... The **first British Empire Games** opened at Hamilton, Canada, in **1930.** The Games were renamed the British Empire and Commonwealth Games in 1954 and the British Commonwealth Games in 1970. The idea of an athletics meeting for the nations of the empire had first been mooted by the Reverend J. Astley Cooper in 1891 ... The legendary baseball player **'Babe' Ruth** died on this day in **1948,** aged 53 (*see 6 February*) ... One half of the Australian pair of demon bowlers in the 1970s, **Jeff Thomson,** was born in **1950.** Together with Dennis Lillee, he was the scourge of English batsmen in the mid seventies. Batsmen found Thomson's strange catapult action difficult to 'read' and his very fast pace unsettling. Thomson took 200 wickets in 51 Tests ... The **New Zealand soccer team** established a World Cup record score at Auckland in **1981** when they beat Fiji 13–0 in a qualifying match. Two days earlier Fiji had lost 10–0 to Australia. They conceded 35 goals in their eight qualifying matches.

**17** In **1919 Gertrude Ederle** became the youngest world record-holder in any sport when, at the age of 12 years and 298 days, she broke the world record in the 880 yards freestyle in Indianapolis.

Seven years later Ederle would become the first woman to swim the English Channel (*see 6 August*) ... In **1928** England and Gloucestershire cricketer **Walter Hammond** took ten catches against Surrey at Cheltenham, a then record by an outfielder in a first-class match ... **Henry Armstrong** beat Lou Ambers on points to win the world lightweight title at New York in **1938** and to become the first man to hold three world titles simultaneously ... The former world middleweight boxing champion **Alan Minter** was born in **1951**. He was the first Briton to win the title since Terry Downes in 1961. Minter outpointed Italian-born Vito Antuofermo for the crown in 1980, only to lose it to 'Marvellous' Marvin Hagler six months later ... Brazilian racing driver **Nelson Piquet** was born in **1952**. He was world champion in 1981, 1983 and 1987 ... Ice skater **Robin Cousins** was born in **1957**. He won both the Olympic and European figure-skating titles in 1980 ... In **1988 Butch Reynolds** broke Lee Evans' 20-year-old world 400 metres record with a time of 43·29 seconds.

## 18

One of England's best-known wicketkeepers, **Godfrey Evans,** was born in **1920**. The Kent 'keeper dismissed 269 batsmen in 95 Test matches, and was the first to claim 200 Test victims ... Jockey **Lester Piggott** enjoyed the sweet smell of success for the first time in **1948**. He piloted The Chase, his seventh ride in public, to victory in the Wigan Lane Selling Handicap over one mile at Haydock. The 10–1 winner was trained by Lester's father, Keith ... In **1990** New Zealand's **All Blacks** suffered their first defeat in nearly four years, losing 21–9 to Australia at Wellington. Their run of 23 successive wins in rugby union internationals stretched back to 22 May 1987 when they beat Italy in the World Cup.

## 19

America's most successful jockey, **Willie Shoemaker,** was born in **1931.** Known as 'The Shoe', he won 11 US Triple Crown races, including four Kentucky Derbys. He rode a record 8833 winners from 40,350 starts between 1949 and his retirement in 1990. A year later he suffered horrific injuries in a car accident which left him severely paralyzed. He continues to train horses despite his disability ... After a gap of 19 years **England** recaptured the Ashes at The Oval in **1953** to end Australia's domination of them. Denis Compton hit the deciding stroke to give Len Hutton's team an eight-wicket victory in the fifth and final Test, the only win after four drawn matches in the series.

## 20

One of the early greats of British lawn tennis, **H. W. 'Bunny' Austin,** was born in **1906.** He was four times a member of the successful British Davis Cup team in the 1930s ... One of the most colourful characters in boxing, promoter **Don King,** was born in **1931.** His first major promotion was Muhammed Ali's comeback fight against Jerry Quarry in 1970. King virtually controlled all world heavyweight title bouts during the reigns of champions Larry Holmes and Mike Tyson. He once served four years in prison for manslaughter (1967–70) and in 1984 was cleared of tax evasion ... Middlesex and England off-spinner **John Emburey** was born in **1952.** He captained England against the West Indian tourists in 1988, replacing the disgraced Mike Gatting. He has played in over 60 Tests ... On this day in **1988 Jack Nicklaus** tied for 34th place in The International at Castle Pines, Colorado, and became the first man to take his career earnings over the $5 million mark on the US PGA Tour ... Having lost 7–4 at home to Crewe on their Football League debut three days earlier in **1991, Barnet** engaged in another goal glut on their League Cup debut, drawing 5–5 with Brentford.

## 21

**Chris Brasher,** the inspiration behind the London Marathon, was born in **1928.** Brasher took the gold medal in the 1956 Olympic steeplechase after a controversial race which first saw him disqualified and then reinstated three hours later. His victory gave Britain its first track and field gold medal for 20 years ... **Gillian Sheen,** another British Olympian who won gold in 1956, was also born in **1928.** She is the only Briton to win a fencing gold medal ... Basketball player **Wilt Chamberlain** was born in **1936.** One of the most prolific scorers in the National Basketball League (NBL), he is the only man to score 100 points in a single game ... In **1965** Charlton's **Keith Peacock** was the first substitute to be used in a Football League game when he came on for Mick Rose against Bolton. The first substitute to score a goal in the League was **Bobby Knox** of Barrow, who came on against Wrexham later in the same day.

## 22

The Royal Yacht Squadron of Great Britain put up the One Hundred Guinea Cup in **1851** as the prize for a race around the Isle of Wight between the American yacht *America* and the British contestant *Aurora.* The Americans won the race and took the trophy back to the United States. In 1870 this prize was offered as a challenge trophy under the name of the America's Cup, now the best-known trophy in international yachting. The Americans dominated the contest before losing it for the first time in 1983 (*see 26 September*) ... Surrey cricketer **Percy Fender,** the man credited with making the fastest century in first-class cricket, was born in **1892** (*see 26 August*) ... The finest snooker player of the modern era, **Steve Davis,** was born in **1957.** He turned professional in 1978 and made an immediate impact on the game. In 1981 he beat Doug Mountjoy for the first of his six world titles. He was the first snooker player to win more than £1 million from the sport ... **BBC TV's *Match of the Day*** showed highlights of the Arsenal—Liverpool match in its first broadcast in **1964.**

## 23

Australian golfer **Peter Thomson** was born in **1929.** He won a post-war record five British Open titles between 1954 and 1965, including three in succession (1954–56). He later found success on the US Seniors' Tour ... **Len Hutton** compiled the highest individual innings in Test cricket against Australia at The Oval in **1938.** His total of 364 runs beat Walter Hammond's old record of 336 not out and stood until 1958 when surpassed by Gary Sobers (*see 1 March*). Hutton's score contributed substantially towards England's total of 903–7 declared (a Test cricket record), which left Australia in arrears to the tune of an innings and 579 runs at the end of the match ... British shotputter **Geoff Capes** was born in **1949.** The 'Gentle Giant', who breeds budgerigars in his spare time, was twice Commonwealth Games champion in the 1970s. His British shotput record was still standing at the start of 1993, 13 years after he set it at

Cwmbran. A former policeman, Capes competed in strongman events after retiring from athletics.

**24**

Scottish golfer **Sam Torrance** was born on this day in **1953**. He will long be remembered by British golf fans for his great play in the Ryder Cup competition in 1985 (*see 15 September*) ... **Jimmy Greaves** made his Football League debut for Chelsea against Tottenham Hotspur in **1957**. He scored, just as he did on his debut for all the teams he played for at club and international level ... **Denise Annetts** of Australia created a women's cricket record in **1987** when she scored 193 runs in the Test against England at Collingham, West Yorkshire.

**25**

In **1875 Captain Matthew Webb** made history as the first man to swim the English Channel. He covered the 21 miles from Dover to Calais in 21 hours and 45 minutes. The current record for the crossing is slightly less than eight hours ... One of the best-known football terraces in the world, the **Spion Kop** at Liverpool's Anfield Road ground, was opened on this day in **1928.** Liverpool celebrated the occasion by beating Bury 3–0 in a first-division game. On the same day in **1928, numbers were worn on the backs of shirts** for the first time in the Football League. The games at Highbury, between first division sides Arsenal and Sheffield Wednesday, and at Stamford Bridge, between second division clubs Chelsea and Swansea Town, were the first to have this novelty. Players were numbered 1–22, with the home team allotted 1–11 and the visitors 12–22. The wearing of numbers became compulsory in 1939 ... In **1964 Worcestershire,** led by Don Kenyon, beat Gloucestershire at

Worcester to win the county cricket championship for the first time ... America's **Carl Lewis** set a new world record for the 100 metres with a time of 9·86 seconds during the world athletics championships at Tokyo in **1991**. Second placed Leroy Burrell also broke the old record, and six of the eight finalists recorded times under ten seconds.

## 26

Surrey batsman **Percy Fender** made the quickest 100 in first-class cricket against Northamptonshire at Northampton in **1920**, rattling off the runs in 35 minutes. His record was equalled by Lancashire's Steven O'Shaughnessy in 1983 (*see 13 September*) ... Showjumper **Malcolm Pyrah** was born in **1941**. Twice winner of the King George V Gold Cup at Wembley, his best known horse was Towerlands Anglezark ... The most tragic **Olympic Games in** living memory opened at Munich in **1972**. The Games were to be marred by the deaths of 11 Israeli athletes at the hands of Arab terrorists.

## 27

One of the greatest batsmen of all time, **Don Bradman,** was born in **1908**. He scored 28,067 runs in first-class cricket between 1927 and 1949 and in 52 Test matches scored 6996 runs at a record 99.94 runs per innings (*see 14 August*) ... British tennis player **John Lloyd** was born in **1954**. He twice won the mixed doubles title at Wimbledon with Australian Wendy Turnbull, but is perhaps better known for his short marriage to the top American player Chris Evert ... English racing driver **Derek Warwick** was also born on this day in **1954** ... German golfer **Bernhard Langer** was born in **1957**. One of the top money-winners in Europe, he won the US Masters in 1985 and

1993 ... Austrian motor-racing driver **Gerhard Berger** was born in **1959** ... In **1990** Graham Gooch scored 88 in England's second innings in the third and final Test against India at The Oval, taking his total in the six Tests that summer to 1058 runs. Sir Donald Bradman's old record of 974 for a series had stood since 1930. Ironically, Gooch set the new record on Bradman's 82nd birthday.

## 28

The former Australian cricket captain **Lindsay Hassett** was born in **1913**. He scored 3073 runs in 43 Tests ... **Emlyn Hughes,** the former Liverpool and England soccer captain, was born in **1947**. The son of a rugby league player, Emlyn was the driving force behind the Liverpool team in the 1970s. He later played for Wolves and won a League Cup winners' medal with them before becoming a radio and television personality. He was captain of the team for which Her Royal Highness Princess Anne played when she appeared on the TV quiz show *A Question of Sport* ... Top American freestyle swimmer **Janet Evans** was born in **1971**. The world record-holder at 400, 800 and 1500 metres freestyle, she won three individual Olympic golds in 1988 and 1992 ... At Brussels in **1981 Sebastian Coe** broke the world mile record for the third time. His time of 3 minutes 47·33 seconds stood until 1985 when it was bettered by Steve Cram (*see 27 July*).

## 29

The forerunner of the Rugby League, the **Northern League,** was born out of a meeting of 21 Lancashire and Yorkshire clubs at the George Hotel, Huddersfield, in **1895**. The members of this breakaway league wanted to make so-called 'broken time' payments to their players for taking time off work to play the game ... British motor-racing driver **James Hunt** was born in **1947.** After starting his formula one career with Hesketh, he teamed up with the Marlboro-McLaren team. In 1976 he captured the world drivers' title by one point from the unfortunate Niki Lauda (*see 24 October*). Hunt died suddenly in 1993 aged 45.

## 30

World heavyweight boxing champion **Joe Louis** was taken the distance in the first of the 25 defences he would make of his title. His opponent on this day in **1937** was Welshman Tommy Farr, who proved the pundits wrong by surviving 15 rounds in the same ring as the 'Brown Bomber' at New York's Madison Square Garden ... French skier **Jean-Claude Killy** was born in **1943.** In 1967 Killy became the first overall World Cup champion as well as winning individual titles in all three disciplines: Downhill, Slalom and Giant Slalom. A year later he won three Winter Olympic golds ... Britain's **Lloyd Honeyghan** knocked out America's Gene Hatcher at Marbella, Spain, in **1987,** to retain his world welterweight title. The knockout was achieved in only 45 seconds, then the shortest world title fight on record (*see 6 September*) ... Bob Beamon's 22-year-old world long-jump record was broken during the world championships in Tokyo in **1991.** Many expected Carl Lewis to break the record, but it was Lewis' team-mate **Mike Powell** who obliged, and in dramatic fashion. Lewis broke Beamon's record with a leap of 8·91 metres (29 feet 2 inches) but this was disallowed because it was wind-assisted. Powell then jumped a massive 8·95 metres (29 feet 3 inches). It was Carl Lewis' first defeat in 66 long-jump competitions going back ten years.

**31**

**Bombardier Billy Wells,** who won 15 British heavyweight boxing title bouts—more than any other man—was born in 1889 ... The **first professional game of US Football** was played on this day in **1895** when Latrobe and Jeanette met in Pennsylvania ... The top Japanese golfer **Isao Aoki** was born in **1942** ... Former West Indian Test cricket captain **Clive Lloyd** was born in **1944.** He scored 7515 runs in 110 Test matches between 1966 and 1985 ... American athlete **Ed Moses** was born in **1955.** The world record-holder for the 400 metres hurdles, he was also the Olympic champion in this event in 1976 and 1984. He once went 122 races without defeat (*see 4 June*) ... French rugby union player **Serge Blanco** was born in **1958.** He won a world record 93 caps between 1980 and 1991, and scored 38 tries ... Cricketing history was made at the St Helens Ground, Swansea, in **1968** when **Gary Sobers** of Nottinghamshire became the first man to score six sixes off one over (*see 28 July*). ... Former world heavyweight boxing champion **Rocky Marciano** died in a plane crash in **1969,** one day short of his 46th birthday (*see 1 September*) ... The former Tottenham Hotspur full-back **Cyril Knowles** died in **1991** at the age of 47 after a long illness. He played 401 games for Spurs between 1964–75 and won four England caps.

# SEPTEMBER

# SEPTEMBER

**1**

Two former world heavyweight boxing champions were born on this day. **James J. Corbett,** known as 'Gentleman Jim', was born in **1866.** He captured the title in 1892 by knocking out John L. Sullivan in the 21st round. He made one successful defence before losing his crown to Bob Fitzsimmons in March 1897. Corbett died in 1933 . . . **'Rocky' Marciano** was born in **1923.** He took the title from 'Jersey Joe' Walcott in 1952. He was undefeated in all 49 of his professional fights, and 43 of these he won inside the distance. He retired in 1956. He was killed in a plane crash the day before his 46th birthday in 1969 . . . On this day in **1972 Bobby Fischer** became the first American to win the world chess championship, defeating Russian Boris Spassky in their much-publicized match at Reykjavik . . . The former Manchester City and Polish international footballer **Kayimerz 'Kaz' Deyna** was killed in a car crash in **1989** at the age of 41. Capped 102 times, he was Poland's captain the day they knocked England out of the World Cup in 1974.

**2**

**Liverpool beat Middlesbrough Ironopolis 2–0** on this day in **1893** to notch up their first win in the Football League. The club has since won more games than any other club in the League and also more League titles (18) . . . American tennis player **Jimmy Connors** was born in **1952.** One of the greats of modern-day tennis, Connors first won Wimbledon as a 21-year-old in 1974 when he destroyed the veteran Australian Ken Rosewall 6–1, 6–1, 6–4. He won his second title eight years later when he beat John McEnroe in a classic five-setter . . . **Ian Botham** played his first game for Somerset on this day in **1973**

when he turned out in a Sunday League game against Sussex at Hove ... **John Arlott,** the 'Voice of Cricket', commentated on his last Test match in **1980,** on the occasion of the Lord's Centenary Match between England and Australia.

**3** **Austria beat Germany 6–3** in the first international handball match in **1925** ... At Bonneville Flats, Utah, in **1935, Malcolm Campbell** became the first man to travel at 300 mph on land when he powered his *Bluebird* to a new world record of 301·13 mph (484·5 km/hr) ... Former New Zealand rugby union captain **Brian Lochore** was born in **1940.** One of the game's great forwards, he played for the All Blacks 25 times between 1964 and 1971 ... In **1950 Giuseppe 'Nino' Farina** won the Italian Grand Prix at Monza in an Alfa Romeo to capture the world title and become the first winner of the newly instituted drivers' championship ... A dramatic finale to the pentathlon at the **1972** Munich Olympics saw Northern Ireland's **Mary Peters** pip West Germany's Heidi Rosendahl to the gold medal by a mere 10 points, 4801 to 4791. The result was in doubt until the final event, the 200 metres, which Peters ran in 24·08 seconds. Had she been one-tenth of a second slower she would have lost the gold medal.

**4** Australia's controversial but brilliant swimmer **Dawn Fraser** was born in **1937.** She is the only swimmer to win gold medals in the same event at three consecutive Olympics: she won the 100 metres freestyle in 1956, 1960 and 1964. She also broke the world record for the event no fewer than nine times ... Two successful American golfers were born on this day. **Raymond**

**Floyd** was born in **1942**. He was the oldest winner of the US Open, at 43 years and 284 days (1986). In 1992 he became the first man to win on both the US Regular and Seniors' Tours in one season ... **Tom Watson** was born in **1949**. He has over 30 US Tour wins to his credit and has won the British Open five times. His four-round total of 268 at Turnberry in 1977 remains a British Open record ... In **1990** Manchester United's **Steve Bruce** became the first player in the first division to receive his marching orders under the new 'professional foul' rule, against Luton Town.

**5**

**John Wisden,** the man who first published what is now known as 'The Cricketer's Bible', was born in **1826**. Wisden played first-class cricket for Sussex but it was as a compiler of cricketing records that he gained far more notoriety. He died in 1884, aged 57 ... **Maureen Connolly,** known affectionately as 'Little Mo', won the **1951** US tennis title at the age of 16 years and 11 months. She was then the youngest winner of the title; Tracy Austin was two months younger when she won the title in 1979 ... **Aston Villa beat Rotherham United 3–0** in the second leg of the inaugural League Cup final in **1961** to win 3–2 on aggregate ... Austrian motor-racing driver **Jochen Rindt** was killed on this day in **1970** when his Lotus swerved and hit a guard rail during practice for the Italian Grand Prix at Monza. Rindt was leading the world championship at the time, six weeks before the end of the season. His points total was not overtaken and he remains the only posthumous world champion in the history of motor racing ... Twelve months later at Monza, in **1971, Peter Gethin** in a BRM took the chequered flag in the closest world championship formula one race in history. He won by one-hundredth of a second from Ronnie Peterson. A mere 0·61 of a second separated the first five cars to finish.

**6** In **1880** the **Kennington Oval** became the first cricket ground in England to host a Test match. England beat Australia by five wickets, with W. G. Grace scoring the first Test century on the ground ... **Frank Stapleton** equalled Don Givens' Republic of Ireland goalscoring record in **1989** when he scored his 19th goal, against West Germany. Stapleton went on to better Givens' record by one goal ... England's first professional Test cricket captain, the great **Sir Leonard Hutton,** died in **1990** at the age of 74 (*see 23 June*) ... **James Warring** took only 24 seconds to knock out James Pritchard in their world cruiserweight contest in **1991**; it is the fastest k.o. in a world boxing title fight.

**7** **James J. Corbett** knocked out John L. Sullivan in the 21st round at the New Orleans Olympic Club in **1892** to become the first world heavyweight champion under Queensberry Rules. Although this claim was disputed some years later, many historians still consider it to be the first such fight ... **Rugby league matches** were first played to the new Northern Union rules in **1895.** Wigan, one of the sport's best known and most successful teams, started their league campaign with a 9–0 win at Broughton Rangers ... All-round sportsman **C. B. Fry** died in **1956** at the age of 84 (*see 25 April*) ... **Sussex,** led by Ted Dexter, beat Worcestershire by 14 runs to win the first one-day cricket final at Lord's in **1963.** Gillette were the sponsors of the competition, which from 1964 to 1980 was known as The Gillette Cup.

**8** The first matches in the newly formed **Football League** were played on this day in 1888. Derby County produced the best result, winning 6–3 at Bolton Wanderers. The other results were: Everton 2 Accrington 1; Preston 5 Burnley 2; Stoke 0 West Brom 2; Wolves 1 Aston Villa 1. The two other founder members of the League, Blackburn and Notts County, did not play. The first champions were Preston North End. They went through the season undefeated and also won the FA Cup without conceding a goal ... **Virginia Wade** beat Billie-Jean King to win the first US Open title in 1968 ... **David Longhurst,** of York City, collapsed and died on the field during a game with Lincoln City in 1990 at the age of 25. He was the first player to die during a Football League game since Sam Wynne of Bury in 1927. Referee Roy Harper collapsed and died while officiating in a game, also at York City's Bootham Crescent ground, in May 1969.

**9** The local 'derby' between **Blackpool and Bolton Wanderers** in 1960 was the first Football League match to be televised live. The match at Bloomfield Road was uninspiring and attracted very little interest. The Football League did not press ahead with the idea and screen more live games. But, of course, that has all changed ... On this day in 1975 the Czechoslovak tennis player **Martina Navratilova** defected to the West. She was granted political asylum in the United States and eventually citizenship. A week earlier the 18-year-old had reached the semifinals of the US Open at Forest Hills ... **Pete Sampras** became the youngest winner of the US Open tennis title in 1990. He was 19 years and one month old when he beat Andre Agassi 6–4, 6–3, 6–2 in the final.

**10** Golfer **Arnold Palmer** was born in **1929.** Palmer was not only a great golfer, and the first to win $1 million, but an inspiration to millions of ordinary people worldwide. His famous Arnold Palmer Driving Ranges helped popularize the game, as did the books that appeared under his name. Palmer was also responsible for getting his fellow American professionals to compete in the British Open in the early-1960s at a time when US interest in the championship was declining. He was rewarded with the title in 1961 and 1962. He won the US masters four times and the Open once, in 1960 . . . Australia's **Lionel Van Praag** won the first world speedway championship, held at Wembley in **1936** . . . On this day in **1962 Rod Laver** beat fellow Australian Roy Emerson in four sets to win the US Championships and complete the Grand Slam. He repeated the feat seven years later . . . **Emerson Fittipaldi** of Brazil won the **1972** Italian Grand Prix at Monza in a Lotus to clinch the world drivers' title. Aged only 25 years and 273 days, he is the youngest-ever world motor-racing champion.

**11** The original **FA Cup trophy** was stolen from the window of William Shillcock's shop at 73 Newtown Row, Birmingham, in **1895;** it had been on display there courtesy of holders Aston Villa. An exact replica of the trophy was made and in 1910 presented to Lord Kinnaird for his services to the FA. A new trophy, the present one, was made by Fattorini & Sons of Bradford, and first played for in 1911. The first winners of this Cup were, coincidently, Bradford City . . . West German footballer **Franz Beckenbauer** was born in **1945.** An outstanding captain, he guided his club, Bayern Munich, to European Cup wins in 1974, 1975 and 1976, and in 1974 led West Germany to victory in the World Cup. He played for the national side 103 times and was twice voted European Footballer of the Year ... Motor cyclist **Barry Sheene** was born in **1950.** World 500cc champion in 1976 and 1977, he won 23 world championship grands prix between 1971 and 1981 and is the only man to win races at 50cc and 500cc.

## 12

On this day in **1885 Arbroath** established a British soccer record when they beat Bon Accord 36–0 in the Scottish FA Cup. Centre-forward John Petrie scored 13 of their goals. On the same day, and in the same competition, Dundee Harp beat Aberdeen Rovers 35–0 ... Athlete **Jesse Owens** was born in **1913.** He once set five world records in one day (*see 25 May*). At the 1936 Berlin Olympics he won four gold medals in the 100 and 200 metres, long jump, and sprint relay ... At the New York Polo Grounds in **1951 'Sugar' Ray Robinson** regained his world welterweight crown by beating Britain's Randolph Turpin in what was billed as 'The Fight of the Century'. Turpin had taken the title from Robinson two months earlier in one of boxing's biggest upsets (*see 10 July*) ... **England** played their first match under Graham Taylor on this day in **1991.** They beat Hungary 1–0 at Wembley thanks to a 44th minute goal from Gary Lineker, who was appointed captain for the first time. Lineker's only previous experience of captaincy had been gained with the Leicestershire Schools cricket team!

**13** The world's first baseball club, the **Knickerbocker Club of New York,** was formed on this day in 1845 ... In **1970 Margaret Court** of Australia beat Rosemary Casals in three sets to win the US Open at Forest Hills and became only the second woman after Maureen Connolly to complete the Grand Slam of the four major tennis championships ... Lancashire's **Steven O'Shaughnessy** scored 100 runs in 35 minutes against Leicestershire at Old Trafford in 1983 to equal the world record for the fastest century in first-class cricket (*see 26 August* ).

**14** **Young Tom Morris** registered the first hole-in-one in the British Open when he aced the 166-yard 8th hole at Prestwick in 1868. Tom went on to beat his father, Old Tom, by three strokes and, at 17, become the youngest winner of the championship ... **John Heath** of Wolverhampton Wanderers converted the first penalty kick in the Football League in a game against Accrington in 1891. Spot kicks had been introduced the previous season by the Irish FA. The Scottish League witnessed its first penalty kick three weeks before Heath's successful conversion ... The **Isle of Man RAC Tourist Trophy,** the oldest surviving motorcar race in the world, was first contested in 1905 ... On this day in **1955 Kidderminster Harriers and Brierley Hill Alliance** made history as the first clubs to contest an FA Cup tie under floodlights ... **George Best,** one of the greatest soccer talents, made his debut for Manchester United against West Bromwich at Old Trafford in 1963. A crowd of 50,453 watched the match, which United won thanks to a goal from David Sadler. It was the first of the 466 games that Best played for United before falling out with the Old Trafford club.

# SEPTEMBER

**15**

In **1976 Derby County** became the first British club to score 12 goals in a European match when they beat Finn Harps of Ireland 12–0 in a UEFA Cup tie. Swansea City equalled this performance in **1982,** beating Malta's Sliema Wanderers by the same score in a Cup-winners' Cup match ... **Lester Piggott** broke Frank Buckle's record of 27 Classic wins when he rode Commanche Run to victory in the **1984** St Leger ... **Tony Jacklin's** team of European golfers inflicted defeat on the Americans in the Ryder Cup for the first time in 28 years at The Belfry in **1985.** The hero of the hour was Sam Torrance, whose play at the 18th in the singles gave him victory over Andy North and assured Europe the Cup. The margin of victory at the end of play was a handsome five points, 16·5 to 11·5.

**16**

**Albert Geldard,** aged 15 years and 158 days, became the youngest-ever player in the Football League when he appeared for Bradford Park Avenue against Millwall in **1929** ... History was made on this day in **1937** when TV cameras covered a specially arranged match between Arsenal's 'firsts' and 'seconds'. The commentary of the **first soccer game to be seen on TV** was shared by 'Mr Boat Race' John Snagge and the Arsenal manager George Allison ... Rugby league stalwart **Roger Millward** was born in **1947.** He made his debut for Great Britain against France in March 1966 at the age of 18 to become the youngest-ever international; a record surpassed by Paul Newlove in 1989. An outstanding player and then coach with Hull Kingston Rovers, he guided the club through one of the most successful periods in its history in the late 1970s to collect the Challenge Cup, Premiership and League title ...

Scottish international rugby union player **Andy Irvine** was born in **1951.** An outstanding full-back, Irvine played for Scotland 51 times and went on three Lions tours, winning nine caps. He scored 301 points in international rugby between 1972 and 1982 and was Scotland's top scorer until surpassed by Gavin Hastings.

# 17

British racing driver **Stirling Moss** was born in **1929.** Moss was unfortunate to reach his peak at the same time as Juan Manuel Fangio of Argentina who held him at bay in the drivers' championship between 1955 and 1957. He also came second in the title race to fellow-Briton Mike Hawthorn in 1958 . . . Tennis player **Maureen Connolly,** known affectionately as 'Little Mo', was born in **1934.** She won Wimbledon on her first attempt, in 1952, and retained the title in 1953 and 1954. In 1953 she became the first women to complete the Grand Slam. She retired in 1955, her career cut short by a riding accident. She died of cancer in 1969 at the age of 34 . . . One of television's top sports presenters, **Desmond Lynam,** was born in **1942.** He moved to BBC television from BBC Radio Two and has gone on to host the top sports programmes, including *Grandstand* and *Sportsnight* . . . **Billy Bonds,** the former West Ham player, and later their manager, was born in **1946.** He played in a record 663 games for the Hammers between 1967 and 1988 . . . Australian batsman **Donald Bradman** played his last innings on British soil at Aberdeen in **1948.** He signed off with a flourish, scoring 123 for Australia against Scotland.

**18**

Snooker player **John Spencer** was born in **1935.** The Lancastrian-born Spencer was world professional champion in 1969, 1971 and 1977. The growth in snooker's popularity in the late 1960s and early 1970s was due largely to Spencer and Welshman Ray Reardon. Spencer was a very talented player whose abundant skills were often overlooked in the rush to acknowledge the new breed of snooker players, such as Steve Davis, emerging on the scene ... The most capped British footballer, **Peter Shilton,** was born in **1949.** He played for his country 125 times and appeared in over 1000 senior games in Britain for Leicester City, Stoke City, Nottingham Forest, Southampton, Derby County and Plymouth Argyle. He took over as manager at Plymouth in 1992.

**19**

Czechoslovak athlete **Emil Zatopek** was born in **1922.** An outstanding distance runner, he won the 10,000 metres at the 1948 London Olympics and at Helsinki four years later took gold in the 5000, 10,000 metres, and Marathon. His wife Dana who, coincidentally, was born on the very same day as Emil in 1922, won gold in the javelin in Helsinki hours after Emil had taken the 5000 metres title ... American tennis player **Rosie Casals** was born in **1948.** A beaten finalist at both Wimbledon and the US Open, this popular competitor had to play second fiddle in the singles to Margaret Court and, especially, Billie-Jean King. She won seven doubles and mixed doubles titles. She was a relative of cellist Pablo Casals.

**20**

The **first organized motor-cycle race** took place on this day in **1896** when eight riders raced the 476 miles (766 km) from Paris to Nantes and back. The winner was M. Chevalier on a Michelin-Dion averaging 22·61 mph (36·38 km/h) ... Race-horse trainer and former National Hunt jockey **Fred Winter** was born in **1926.** His illustrious career as a jump-jockey included two Grand National wins, on Sundew in 1957 and Kilmore in 1962, two Cheltenham Gold Cups and three Champion Hurdles. He was top NH Trainer eight times between 1971 and 1985 ... **Chris Marron** of South Shields scored ten goals against Radcliffe Borough in an FA Cup qualifying round match in **1947,** a competition record which still stands ... **Terry Fenwick** of Tottenham Hotspur was jailed for four months on a drink-drive charge in **1991** ... **Ray Floyd** won the GTE North Classic on the US Seniors' Golf Tour in **1992,** only the second Seniors' event Floyd had entered. Floyd had already won the Doral Ryder Open on the Regular Tour six months earlier and so this victory meant he was the first man to win on both the Regular and Seniors' Tour in the same season.

**21**

The former West Indian cricketer **Sir Learie Constantine** was born in **1902.** The former High Commissioner for Trinidad and Tobago, he became Britain's first black peer in 1969. Sir Learie played for the West Indies 18 times and is one of the few men to perform the hat-trick and score a century in a first-class match which he did against Northants in 1928. He died in 1971, aged 68 ... The **Republic of Ireland beat England 2–0** at Goodison Park, Everton, in **1949** to inflict a first defeat on the home side by a visiting team from outside the United Kingdom ... **Rocky**

**Marciano** knocked out Archie Moore in the ninth round of their title fight at New York's Yankee Stadium in **1955** to retain his world heavyweight crown. This was the last of Marciano's 49 professional fights and his sixth title defence. He announced his retirement seven months later. He remains the only former world heavyweight champion to end his professional career with a 100 per cent record: 49 fights, 49 wins ... **Richard Todd** threw an NFL record 42 completed passes during a game for the New York Jets against the San Francisco 49ers in **1980.**

## 22

The famous **'Battle of the Long Count'** occurred during the Jack Dempsey-Gene Tunney world heavyweight title fight at Soldier Field, Chicago, in **1927.** The bout was a return, Dempsey having lost his title to Tunney exactly twelve months earlier (*see 23 September*). A crowd of over 100,000 paid $2·5 million to see the fight, which turned into one of the most controversial in boxing history. In the seventh round Dempsey sent Tunney crashing to the canvas and then stood over his prostrate opponent. Referee Dave Barry refused to start the count until Dempsey had retreated to a neutral corner. Dempsey, unaware of the Illinois State Athletic Commission rule which required him to do this, eventually complied. The delay to the start of the count meant that Tunney was on the canvas for around 15 seconds, enough time for him to collect his wits and get to his feet. Tunney went on to win the fight on points and prevent Dempsey becoming the first man to regain the title. Dempsey said afterwards that he had been 'robbed of the championship'.

## 23

The **first set of baseball rules** were drawn up by Alexander Joy Cartwright jnr in **1845** ... The world heavyweight boxing contest between **Gene Tunney and Jack Dempsey** at the Sesquicentennial Stadium, Philadelphia, in **1926** attracted 120,757 spectators, the largest crowd ever seen at a boxing match. Tunney won the title on points over ten rounds ... In **1952 Rocky Marciano** won the world heavyweight title, knocking out the defending champion, 'Jersey Joe' Walcott, in the 13th round at the Municipal Stadium, Pennsylvania (*see 21 September*) ... **Liverpool** equalled the Football League Cup record by beating Fulham 10–0 in the first leg of their second-round tie in **1986.** The Fulham officials included the following note in the programme for the second leg: 'In the event of the scores being level after tonight's game the replay will be on...' That's optimism (*see 25 October*).

## 24

The **St Leger** was run for the first time in **1776,** at Doncaster. The oldest of the five Classic races, the first St Leger was won by the 2–1 favourite Allabucilia, ridden by J. Singleton. There were only five runners. The race is named after Anthony St Leger, the leader of the City Fathers of Doncaster, who came up with the idea ... **Lottie (Charlotte) Dod,** the youngest Wimbledon champion at 15 years and 10 months, was born in **1871.** She won the ladies' singles title five times, in 1887–88 and 1891–93. She gave up tennis at the age of 21 to concentrate on golf, and became British Women's Champion at Troon in 1904. She was also a first-rate archer and an international hockey player ... **Jim Bakken** kicked an NFL record seven field goals in a game while playing for St Louis against Pittsburgh in

**1967** ... In **1975 Phil Bennett** scored an international rugby union record 34 points for Wales against Japan in Tokyo ... At the Seoul Olympics in **1988** Canadian sprinter **Ben Johnson** 'won' the 100 metres in a world record time of 9·79 seconds. The record was disallowed and the medal taken from him when drug tests proved that he had taken performance-boosting anabolic steroids ... **Europe** retained the Ryder Cup in **1989** following a 14–14 draw with the United States at The Belfry; it was only the second tied match in the Cup's history. Tom Kite of America registered the biggest individual win in the competition over 18 holes—only since 1961 have all matches been played over this number—by beating Howard Clark 8 and 7.

## 25

The former Indian Test cricket captain **Bishen Bedi** was born in **1946.** He is second only to Kapil Dev as India's most prolific wicket taker with 266 victims in 67 Tests to his credit ... The giant **Sonny Liston** knocked out Floyd Patterson in the first round of their world heavyweight contest at Comiskey Park, Chicago, in **1962.** Patterson, conceding 26 lb (11·8 kg) in weight to the challenger, was the first man to lose the heavyweight title in the first round. The re-match ten months later followed the same pattern with Liston again winning in the opening round ... **Nelson Piquet** beat Alain Prost and Nigel Mansell to the chequered flag in the first European Grand Prix at Brands Hatch in **1983,** a new event in the schedule of world championship races.

**26** Australian Test cricketer **Ian Chappell** was born in **1943.** The older Brother of Greg, Ian enjoyed a successful Test career until 1977 when he became skipper of one of Kerry Packer's breakaway teams. Ian appeared in 75 Tests, 71 of them consecutively. He scored 5345 runs at an average of 42·42. Against New Zealand at Wellington in 1973 he joined that select band of players to score two centuries in the same Test match. Brother Greg uniquely also scored two centuries in the same match ... In beating Anderlecht 10–0 in the European Cup in **1956 Manchester United** became the first British club to score ten goals in a match in one of the three major European club tournaments ... The **first two matches in the Football League Cup** competition, which has since been known by many other names, were played on this day in **1960.** Bristol Rovers beat Fulham 2–1 and West Ham beat Charlton Athletic 3–1 ... **Franz Beckenbauer,** Germany's finest-ever football captain, made his international debut in a 2–1 win over Sweden in **1965.** He would win a further 102 caps in his illustrious career ... The longest winning streak in any sport ended on this day in **1983** when *Australia II,* skippered by John Bertrand, captured the America's Cup from the US yacht *Liberty,* with Dennis Conner at the helm, at Newport, Rhode Island. The trophy, originally called the One Thousand Guinea Cup, had been in the hands of the New York Yacht Club since the competition was inaugurated in 1851.

**27** The most amazing 'grand slam' in golfing history was completed on this day in **1930.** Amateur golfer **Bobby Jones** had already won the British Amateur Championship at St Andrews, the British Open at Hoylake and the US Open at Minneapolis when he made his way to Merion for the US Amateur Championship. He registered easy wins in his first four matches and then dispatched Eugene Homans emphatically 8 and 7 in the final to win the title and earn him a unique Grand Slam. No man is likely to come near to equalling this record ... The most successful player in either men's or women's golf, **Kathy Whitworth,** was born in **1939.** She won 88 events on the US Ladies Tour, including six Majors. The US Women's Open eluded her, however. The most successful men's golfer, Sam Snead, also failed to capture the US Open ... **Joe Louis'** attempt to regain the world heavyweight title 18 months after announcing his retirement ended in a points defeat by Ezzard Charles at the Yankee Stadium in **1950** ... The **European Ryder Cup** team made history at Muirfield Village, Ohio, in **1987** when they became the first to beat the US team on home soil since the tournament began in 1927. Under the leadership of their non-playing captain, Tony Jacklin, Europe retained the trophy with a 15–13 win. Eamonn Darcy's victory over the putter-less Ben Crenshaw sealed victory for the Europeans.

## 28

A great horseracing career was launched on this day in **1870** when 13-year-old **Fred Archer** rode his first winner, partnering Athol Daisy to victory at Chesterfield. It was the first of 2748 winners for Archer whose all-too-brief career ended in suicide at the age of 29 (*see 8 November*) ... **Norm Van Brocklin** set an NFL record in **1951** when he passed for 554 yards (506·5 m) playing for the Los Angeles Rams against the New York Yanks ... Britain's **Lloyd Honeyghan** stopped champion Donald

Curry at Atlantic City in **1986** to win the world welterweight title and become the first British holder of the title since John H. Stracey in 1976.

**29**

West Indian cricketer **Lance Gibbs** was born in **1934.** He claimed a total of 309 victims in 79 Tests between 1958 and 1976. Gibbs was only the second man in cricket history to take 300 Test wickets; Freddie Trueman was the first . . . British speed ace **John Cobb** was killed on this day in **1952** when his jet-engined *Crusader* disintegrated on Loch Ness . . . Former Welsh rugby captain and fly-half **Gareth Davies** was born in **1956.** His international career looked over in 1982 when the selectors blamed him for Wales' defeat by Scotland. He earned a recall three years later and won 21 caps before eventually retiring . . . **Sebastian Coe** was born on the same day as Gareth Davies in **1956.** Probably Britain's greatest middle-distance runner, he set individual world records at 800, 1000, 1500 metres and the mile between 1979 and 1981. He won the Olympic 1500 metres title in 1980 and 1984 and also took silver in the 800 metres at both Games . . . **Chelsea** beat the **Luxembourg club Jeunesse Hautcharage 8–0** in the first leg of their Cup-winners' Cup encounter in **1971** and then demolished them 13–0 in the second leg at Stamford Bridge; the 21–0 aggregate is a European record . . . Liverpool mourned one of its most famous 'adopted' sons in **1981** when the legendary **Bill Shankly** died. Shankly took Liverpool out of the second division in 1962 and turned them into one of the best and most feared teams in the world. He laid the foundations on which all subsequent Liverpool managers have built their teams and continued the club's success.

## 30

All 11 players in the **Belgium football team** facing Holland on this day in **1964** were from the same club, Anderlecht. This was the first time in the history of the game that places in a national side have been filled entirely by players from one professional club ... On this day in **1984** bookmakers William Hill paid out the largest odds when they paid a Hampshire punter the equivalent of 1·67 million to one for a 5p bet. He correctly forecast all seven winners in the ITV 7.

# OCTOBER

# OCTOBER

**1** Footballer **Duncan Edwards,** potentially one of the greatest of all time, was born in **1936.** A member of Matt Busby's gifted Manchester United team, he was the youngest England international this century when he made his debut, aged 18, against Scotland in 1955. He died of injuries received in the Munich Air Disaster (*see 21 February*) ... The **first competitive soccer match played under floodlights** in Britain was a Football Combination game between Southampton reserves and Tottenham Hotspur reserves at The Dell in **1951** ... On this day in **1975 Joe Frazier and Muhammad Ali** did battle in the much publicized 'Thrilla in Manila' bout to decide the heavyweight title. It was the third meeting between the two men and with the score standing at 1–1 a lot of pride was at stake. Ali, the defending champion, emerged the victor at the end of 14 rounds when Frazier was not allowed out of his corner for the final round. One of the most unrelenting heavyweight contests ever seen, the 'thrilla' lived up to its pre-fight billing.

**2** The **first rugby match at Twickenham** was played in **1909** when resident club Harlequins lined up against Richmond. Known as 'Billy Williams' Cabbage Patch' because it is built on the site of a market garden, it is the home of the Rugby Football Union ... In the **1968** World Series **Robert Gibson** of St Louis Cardinals pitched a championship record 17 strikeouts against the Detroit Tigers. The Tigers won the best-of-seven series 4–3 despite Gibson's heroic achievement ... The great Finnish long-distance runner **Paavo Nurmi** died in **1973** aged 76 (*see 13 June*) ... Three times world heavyweight boxing champion **Muhammad Ali** had his 25th and last world heavyweight title fight in **1980** at Caesar's Palace in Las Vegas when he was stopped by champion Larry Holmes in the 10th round ... The **Wimbledon–Sheffield Wednesday** game at Selhurst Park in **1991** attracted a gate of only 3121, the lowest at a first-division game since the war.

**3** The **first inter-county women's cricket match** took place in **1811** when Hampshire and Surrey played each other at Newington ... One of Australia's great post-war fast bowlers, **Ray Lindwall,** was born in **1921.** A former Test captain, he took 228 wickets in 61 Tests between 1946 and 1960; exactly half of them, 114, were against England ... American golfer **Fred Couples** was born in **1959.** A professional since 1980, he has been one of the most consistent golfers in the 1990s. In 1992 he captured his first Major, beating Ray Floyd by two strokes to win the US Masters.

**4** The **first US Open golf championship** took place at Newport, Rhode Island, in **1895.** The winner of the $150 first prize was English-born Horace Rawlins with a score of 173 (91 and 82) ... South African cricketer **Basil d'Oliveira** was born in **1931.** The Worcestershire and England batsman was at the centre of a controversy when dropped from the side to tour his home country in 1964–65 because of his opposition to South Africa's apartheid policies. When the MCC did finally pick him for a tour to his troubled homeland, in 1968, the South African authorities reacted by cancelling the series. He played for England 44 times ... **Gordon Richards** rode all six winners on the card on the first day of two at Chepstow in **1933.** Richards had won the last race at the Nottingham meeting on the previous day. Remarkably the day after his coup at Chepstow he rode the first five winners of the day to take his sequence to a staggering 12 consecutive victories. His run ended in the 4.30 at Chepstow when his mount Eagle Ray finished third ... Speedway star **Ivan Mauger** was born in **1939.** The New Zealand rider has won more individual world titles than any other man, six between 1968 and 1979 ... Former England Test cricket captain **Norman Yardley** died in **1989** at the age of 74 (*see 19 March*) ... **Peter Taylor,** Brian Clough's former right-hand man, died at the age of 62 while holidaying in Majorca in **1991.** They shared the managerial roles at Hartlepool, Derby and Brighton football clubs before falling out and going their separate ways.

**5** **Newcastle United** equalled the Football League record for the biggest winning margin when they thrashed Newport County 13–0 in a second-division game in **1946** (*see 6 January*) ... Scotland's most capped scrum-half, **Roy Laidlaw,** was born in **1953.** He won 47 caps between 1980 and 1988 ... The **British Ryder Cup team,** led by Dai Rees, beat the Americans at Lindrick in **1957** to register their first win since 1933. The Americans would not lose again until 1985 (*see 15 September*) ... In **1965** the leading ice hockey player **Mario Lemieux** was born. He equalled the Stanley Cup record of five goals in a match for Pittsburgh against Philadelphia in 1989.

**6** A busy day for birthdays ... American tennis champion **Helen Wills-Moody** was born in **1905.** Her total of 31 Grand Slam titles included 19 in the singles, eight of them in the ladies' championship at Wimbledon ... Former England centre-forward **Tommy Lawton** was born in **1919.** He scored 22 goals in 23 full internationals ... In **1926** the New York Yankees' **'Babe' Ruth** became the first batter to hit three home runs in a World Series game (*see 9 October*) ... Australian cricketer **Richie Benaud** was born in **1930.** A great all-rounder, he scored 2201 Test runs and took 248 wickets. He later found fame as a cricket commentator ... **Tony Greig** was born on this day in **1946.** South African-born Greig captained England before joining Kerry Packer's rebels in the 1970s ... Liverpool goalkeeper **Bruce Grobbelaar,** known as 'The Clown Prince of Goal-keepers', was born in **1957.** South African-born Grobbelaar started his career in the Football League with Crewe ... A record 92,706 fans watched the fifth game of the **1959 World Series** between the Dodgers and the White Sox at the Los Angeles Coliseum ... **Walter Hagen,** one of America's most flamboyant golfers, died in **1969** at the age of 76 (*see 21 December*) ... **Nigel Mansell,** driving a Williams, notched up his first win in formula one in the European Grand Prix at Brands Hatch in **1985.**

**7** **Lyudmilla Touroscheva,** one of the most elegant of all the great Soviet gymnasts, was born in **1952.** Her total of 34 Olympic, World and European Championship medals exceeds by two the number won by the great Czech gymnast Vera Caslavska. Touroscheva won four Olympic golds in 1968, 1972 and 1976 ... **Jayne Torvill,** the other half of Britain's best-ever ice-dance team, was born in **1957.** She and Christopher Dean won the world title four years in succession between 1981 and

1984. They also won a record six British titles between 1978 and 1983 and gold at the 1984 Olympics.

**8** **Miss Eileen Joel,** daughter of the millionaire racehorse owner Jim Joel, made history at Newmarket in **1925** as the first woman jockey to win an 'open' race, the four-mile Town Plate, on Hogier. The race, which dates to 1665, is open to any rider irrespective of sex. Five of the eight jockeys in the 1925 race were women ... The former Australian Test cricket captain **Neil Harvey** was born in **1928.** A prolific batsman, he scored 6149 runs in 79 Tests and is the fourth top-scoring Australian in Test cricket ... Welsh snooker player **Ray Reardon** was born in **1932.** Winner of six world titles between 1970 and 1978, four of them in successive years (1973–76), Reardon was one of the great personalities of the game and played a major role in developing the sport in the 1970s. In addition to winning the world title, Reardon captured most of the other major titles open to professionals in those 'pioneering' days. Although he has slipped down the world rankings, he continues to entertain people at exhibition evenings and remains very popular ... American swimmer **Matt Biondi** was born in **1955.** Four times holder of the world 100 metres freestyle record, Biondi won seven medals at the 1988 Olympics including five gold. In three Olympics (1984–92) he won 11 medals: eight gold, two silver and one bronze.

**9** Two years after becoming the first man to hit three home runs in a World Series game, in **1928 'Babe' Ruth** repeated the feat, hitting three 'homers' against the St Louis Cardinals, the same team who were on the receiving end in 1926. This time, however, Ruth's contribution helped the Yankees clinch the best-of-seven series 4–0 and take the most cherished prize in baseball ... Middle-distance runner **Steve Ovett** was born in **1955.** He and his great rival Sebastian Coe dominated the 800 metres, 1500 metres and mile in the late 1970s and early 1980s. Ovett pipped Coe to win the Olympic 800 metres title in 1980. Two years earlier Ovett captured the European Championship 1500 metres title. He broke the 1500 metres world record three times and twice broke the mile record ... **Jackie Milburn,** one of Newcastle United's best known footballers and the uncle of Jackie and Bobby Charlton, died in **1988** at the age of 64. Milburn scored both goals in Newcastle's 2–0 win over Blackpool in the 1951 FA Cup final. And he set up Newcastle's 3–1 win over Manchester City in the 1955 final by scoring the first after a little over a minute (*see 11 May*).

**10**

The **XVIIIth Olympics** opened in Tokyo in **1964.** More than 5000 competitors from 93 nations took part in the Games which ended with the United States and Soviet Union topping the medal chart, followed by the host nation in third place with 16 golds. It was the first time that sex tests for women athletes were used at the Games ... The Arsenal and England defender **Tony Adams** was born in **1966.** He came through the junior ranks at Arsenal, eventually breaking into the first team in the 1980s when the club was re-establishing itself at the top of the first division. He has won FA Cup, League Cup and League Championship honours with the Gunners and in 1987 was picked to play for England ... The inaugural meeting of soccer's newly formed **Premier League** was held in 1991 with the former first division clubs seeking to formulate its rules and constitution.

## 11

England's most prolific goalscorer, **Bobby Charlton,** was born in 1937. The scorer of a record 49 goals for England, Bobby played for his country 106 times. He played in 644 Football League games for Manchester United and Preston and was the United captain the day they beat Benfica to become the first English winners of the European Cup. At the end of his playing days he became manager of Preston North End ... Brazilian-born tennis player **Maria Bueno** was born in 1939. The 'Darling' of the centre court in the 1960s, she first won Wimbledon as a 20-year-old in 1959. She retained the title in 1960 and regained it in 1964. She also won the US title four times ... British hurdler **Alan Pascoe** was born on this day in 1947. He was the European 400 metres hurdles champion in 1974. He won a silver medal in the relay at the 1972 Munich Olympics ... **Henry Morris** of East Fife scored the first goal by a British player in a World Cup match, in 1949. The match, between Scotland and Northern Ireland at Belfast, was a qualifier for the 1950 tournament. Morris completed a hat-trick in the match and yet never played for Scotland again! Scotland won the game 8–2.

## 12

Czechoslovak-born tennis player **Jaroslav Drobny** was born in 1921. His first success in sport came in 1948 when he won a silver medal with the Czech ice hockey team at the Winter Olympics. His career as a tennis player flourished after he sought and gained political asylum in Egypt in 1949. He first played at

Wimbledon in 1938, was a beaten finalist in 1949 and 1952 and, finally, in 1954, won the title. The final, against Australian Ken Rosewall, was a marathon four-setter, 13–11, 4–6, 6–2, 9–7. He also won the French Open title twice, in 1951 and 1952 ... At the Sunrise Golf Club, Las Vegas, in **1991 Chip Beck** equalled the US PGA Tour record for 18 holes, set by Al Geiberger 14 years earlier, by shooting a 59 in the third round of the Las Vegas Invitational (*see 10 June*).

**13**

On this day in **1894 Everton and Liverpool** played the first-ever Merseyside 'Derby', at Goodison Park. Everton won the match 3–0. Liverpool have forged ahead in the series since then: of their 154 League meetings between 1894 and the start of the 1993–94 season, Liverpool have won 59 times to Everton's 50 ... **Benny Lynch** retained his world flyweight title at Clyde's Shawfield Stadium in **1937** with a 13th-round knockout of fellow-Briton Peter Kane. The contest is regarded as one of the finest flyweight contests of all time ... On this day in **1954** Britain's **Chris Chataway** knocked a staggering five seconds off the world 5000 metres record, clocking a time of 13 minutes 15·6 seconds in beating the great Russian Vladimir Kuts at London's White City ... Cuban high-jumper **Javier Sotomayor** was born in **1967**. The 1992 Olympic gold medal winner was the first man to clear eight feet (2·44 m), in 1989 (*see 29 July*) ... **John Lowe** made the first nine-dart finish in a major championship at Slough during the quarter-finals of the British Open darts championship in **1984,** to collect a record prize of £102,000. His score of 501 was achieved with six treble-20s, treble-17, treble-18 and double-18 ... **West Indies** scored a cricket World Cup record 360–4 against Sri Lanka at Karachi in **1987.** In the match Viv Richards scored a World Cup best individual innings of 181.

## 14

The **first football match to be played under floodlights** was staged on this day in **1878** at Bramall Lane, Sheffield, between two local teams. Two portable generators provided power for four beams which gave out light equivalent to 30,000 candles. A crowd of 2000 watched the game ... **Steve Cram,** the British middle-distance runner, was born in **1960.** He set world records at 2000 metres and one mile. His mile record of 3 minutes 46·32 seconds set at Oslo in 1985 still stood in August 1993.

## 15

Heavyweight boxing champion **John L. Sullivan,** known as 'The Boston Strong Boy', was born in **1858.** The world bare-knuckle champion from 1882 to 1892, he failed in his attempt to become the first heavyweight champion under Queensberry rules, losing to James J. Corbett by a knockout in the 21st round at New Orleans in 1892 (*see 7 September*) ... On this day in **1887** **Preston North End** established the highest score in senior English soccer when they beat Hyde United 26–0 in a first round FA Cup tie. Centre-forward Jimmy Ross scored eight goals ... Millions of British TV viewers watched **David Hemery** win the Olympic 400 metres hurdles title to the strains of an excited David Coleman on this day in **1968** ... **Nick Faldo** beat Ian Woosnam by one hole to win the Suntory World Matchplay Championship at Wentworth in **1990.** Faldo gave his £100,000 winnings, the largest prize in a British golf tournament, to a children's charity ... On the same day in **1990, UEFA** announced that Wrexham had to set off 24 hours before their Cup-winners' Cup tie with Manchester United to comply with UEFA rules, although the journey up the M56 would take just 40 minutes by coach!

## 16

Jockey **Gordon Richards** had his first ride, at Lingfield Park in **1920.** In a 21,843-race career that lasted until 1954, he won a record 4870 races, 14 of them Classics, and was champion jockey a record 26 times ... Popular Welsh snooker player **Terry Griffiths** was born in **1947.** He beat his great friend and rival Dennis Taylor to win the world championship in 1979. Griffiths has remained near the top of the world rankings since that surprise win and is one of the biggest money-winners in the sport ... It was quite a day in the track and field events at the **1968** Olympics: Britain's **Lillian Board** was pipped by the French girl Colette Besson in the 400 metres final; US sprinters **Tommie Smith and John Carlos** gave their 'Black Power' salute on the winners' rostrum; and in the most thrilling pole vault contest seen at the Olympics, the three medallists—**Bob Seagren** of the US and the Germans **Claus Schiprowski** and **Wolfgang Nordwig**—registered the same height, 5·40 (17 feet 7 inches).

## 17

The **first British Open golf championship** was played at Prestwick in **1860.** Eight men contested the event over three rounds of the 12-hole course. The competition, which was completed in one day, was won by Willie Park senior with a total of 174 strokes. The pre-tournament favourite, Old Tom Morris, was runner-up ... The BBC's top boxing commentator **Harry**

**Carpenter** was born in 1925 . . . British tennis and table tennis player **Ann Jones** was born in **1938.** As Ann Haydon she won the British table tennis title and was twice runner-up in the world championships. She changed sports and in 1967 was beaten by Billie-Jean King in the Wimbledon singles final. Two years later she avenged that defeat, beating King in three sets to become only the second Briton since the 1939–45 war to win a Wimbledon singles title (*see 4 July*) . . . Wigan and Great Britain rugby league player **Shaun Edwards** was born in **1966.** He signed for Wigan for a £35,000 signing-on fee on his 17th birthday and in his first season became the youngest person to appear in the Challenge Cup final.

**18**

At a meeting on this day in **1871,** 12 teams agreed to inaugurate the **FA Cup competition** suggested by FA secretary Charles Allcock . . . **Martina Navratilova** was born in **1956.** She won an all-time record nine Wimbledon singles titles between 1978 and 1990. Add to that another nine singles titles won in the US, Australian and French championships and 36 Grand Slam doubles titles and she must rank as one of the all-time greats. In 1993 she surpassed Chris Evert's record of 157 tournament wins . . . Boxer **Tommy Hearns** was born in **1958.** The first boxer to win world titles in four different weight divisions, he went on to win a fifth title following the formation of the WBO. He held the WBA welterweight, the WBC junior-middleweight, light-heavyweight and middleweight titles and the WBO super-middleweight title . . . One of the greatest of all track and field achievements took place on this day in **1968** when American **Bob Beamon** shattered the world long-jump record by a staggering $21\frac{3}{4}$ inches (55·24 cm) to set a new mark at 29 feet $2\frac{1}{2}$ inches (8·9 m). His record by-passed the 28-foot (8·5 m) mark completely and stood for nearly 23 years (*see 10 November*).

## 19

This day in **1957** is one that supporters of Glasgow Rangers try to forget: their team was trounced 7–1 by rivals **Celtic** in the final of the Scottish League Cup at Hampden Park. John McPhail was the Celtic hero with three goals . . .In **1958 Stirling Moss** beat Mike Hawthorn in the one and only Moroccan Grand Prix. Second place was enough to give Hawthorn, who drove for Ferrari, the world title by one point and consign Moss to the runner-up slot for the fourth consecutive year. The points system was such that Hawthorn captured the title despite winning only one race all season while Moss won four. In those days only the best six results counted, with 8 points for the winner and 6 for the runner-up and so on. A point was also awarded to the driver of the fastest lap. Hawthorn retired soon after becoming world champion and was killed in a car crash near his Surrey home a few months later . . . The former world heavyweight boxing champion **Evander Holyfield** was born in **1962.** He became the world cruiserweight champion in 1986 by beating Dwight Qawi. In 1990 he beat James 'Buster' Douglas to win the heavyweight title. His first defeat in 29 professional fights was by Riddick Bowe who took the heavyweight crown from him in November 1992.

## 20

Liverpool and Wales footballer **Ian Rush** was born in **1961.** The Liverpool manager Bob Paisley had no hesitation in paying £300,000 for the inexperienced youngster, who had only a handful of games for Chester under his belt before he moved to Merseyside. Paisley's confidence has been totally vindicated: Rush has played over 400 games for Liverpool and has surpassed Roger Hunt's goalscoring record for the club. A brief spell in Italy with Juventus did not work out and Liverpool had no hesitation in taking him back to Anfield. On his 29th birthday, in 1990, he appeared in his 500th senior domestic game, against Norwich at Carrow Road. Unfortunately, he did not make it a triple celebration by finding the net. On the same day in 1990 21 **Arsenal and Manchester United** players were involved in a brawl at Old Trafford (*see 12 November*).

## 21

The former Yorkshire and England batsman **Geoffrey Boycott** was born in 1940. Controversial at times, but brilliant at others, Boycott scored a one-time world record 8114 runs in 108 Tests between 1964 and 1982. He scored a total of 48,426 runs in his first-class career, and averaged 56·83 per innings. He is the only man whose average in a season twice exceeded 100 runs ... Top Australian rugby union player **David Campese** was born in 1962. He has played more than 70 games for his country since making his debut in 1982. In 1992 he scored a record-breaking 50th try in international rugby. He scored six tries during Australia's successful World Cup campaign in 1991 ... **Greta Waitz** of Norway became the first woman to run a marathon in under 2 hours 30 minutes when she clocked a time of 2 hours 27 minutes 33 seconds in the 1979 New York City Marathon. Waitz won the race nine times between 1978 and 1988 ... Second place in the final race of the 1984 season, the Portuguese Grand Prix, gave Austrian **Niki Lauda** the world motor-racing championship for the third time. The man who won the race, Lauda's McLaren team-mate Alain Prost, was pipped to the title by the narrowest of margins, just half a point.

## 22

**Broughton and Swinton** played in the first floodlit rugby match on this day in 1878 ... **George Cohen,** full-back, and member of the England 1966 World Cup winning team, was born in 1939 ... Racehorse trainer **Michael Stoute** was born in 1945. In the 1989 season his horses won a record £2 million in prize-money ... In 1966 **David Bryant** won the singles title at the inaugural World Bowls Championship in Sydney. The championship was organized because the sport had been left out of that year's Commonwealth Games in Kingston, Jamaica ... The career of England and Stoke City goalkeeper **Gordon Banks** was cut short in 1972 when he lost an eye following a car crash near his home in Staffordshire. He played in his last Football League game on the day before the accident, away to Liverpool at Anfield. Stoke lost 2–1.

## 23

**Douglas Jardine,** the England Test cricket captain at the centre of the 'bodyline' controversy in 1932–33, was born in 1900. He died in 1958, aged 57 (*see 17 January*) ... **Gertrude Ederle,** the first woman to swim the English Channel, was born in 1906 ... **William Gilbert 'W. G.' Grace** died on this day in 1915 at the age of 67 (*see 18 July*) ... The world's greatest footballer, **Pelé,** was born in 1940. Born Edson Arantes do Nascimento, he appeared in 1363 first-class matches, including 111 for Brazil. He scored 1281 first-class goals, 97 of them at international level. After a successful career in Brazil he moved to North

America where soccer fans packed stadiums to see the greatest footballer of all time ... **Lester Piggott** was jailed on this day in **1987** for income tax offences. He was released after serving a third of his three-year sentence ... **Henry Armstrong,** the only boxer to hold world titles at three different weights simultaneously, died on this day in **1988** (*see 12 December*).

## 24

The first football team, **Sheffield FC,** was formed at a meeting of Cambridge University old boys in **1857** ... The 1977 British Lions tour captain **Phil Bennett** was born in **1948.** He played for the Lions in eight Tests and for Wales on 29 occasions. His 34 points for Wales against Japan in 1975 is an international record ... Australian golfer **Ian Baker-Finch** was born in **1960.** A professional since 1979, he has been successful on the US Tour. His greatest moment to date came at Birkdale in 1991 when he won the British Open ... **James Hunt's** third place in the Japanese Grand Prix at Fuji in **1976** was good enough to secure him the world title by one point from Niki Lauda, who quit on lap two because torrential rain had made conditions too dangerous for his liking. Lauda's caution was understandable given the horrific injuries he had suffered 11 weeks earlier (*see 22 February*) ... In **1987** 37-year-old **Joe Bugner's** attempt to regain the British heavyweight title was thwarted in the eighth round by defending champion Frank Bruno. The pre-match hype for the fight at Tottenham Hotspur's White Hart Lane ground was considerably better than the fight itself.

**25**

The East German swimmer **Kornelia Ender** was born in **1958.** At the **1976** Montreal Olympics she became the first woman to win four swimming gold medals at one Games; all were in world record times. She set a staggering 23 world records between 1973 and 1976 . . . In **1983 West Ham** became the first team to score 10 goals in a match in the Football League Cup, beating Bury 10–0 in the second leg of their second round encounter . . . **Frankie Bunn** of Oldham Athletic set a League Cup individual record in **1989** when he scored six against Scarborough . . . In the final of the Sharjah Cup in **1991 Aaqib Javed** of Pakistan produced the best bowling figures in a one-day cricket international by dismissing seven Indian batsmen for 37 runs, including a hat-trick.

**26**

The **Football Association** was formed on this day in **1863** following a meeting of 11 representatives from interested clubs at the Freemasons Tavern, Lincoln's Inn Fields, London . . . The highest scoring game in Scotland's top division was played on this day in **1895, Celtic beating Dundee 11–0** . . . The heaviest man to hold the world heavyweight boxing title, **Primo Carnera** of Italy, was born in **1906.** He won the title from Jack Sharkey in 1933. When he made his second defence against Tommy Loughran in 1934 Carnera weighed in at a record 270 pounds (122·7 kg); Loughran weighed just 184 pounds (83·6 kg). The weight difference of 86 pounds (39 kg) is the greatest between contestants in a world title fight. Carnera lost his title to American Max Baer in New York in June 1934. He died aged 60 in 1967 . . . A **Brian Kilcline** own goal was enough to give Leeds United a 1–0 home win over Oldham Athletic at

Elland Road in **1991** and put them at the top of the first division for the first time since the days of Don Revie 17 years earlier. Leeds shared the top spot with Manchester United throughout most of the season but finally won the title in a tense finish.

**27** The most successful bowls player in modern times, **David Bryant,** was born in **1931.** Somerset-born Bryant won the first outdoor world championship in 1966. He won the singles on two more occasions and also won triples and team gold medals. He also won the world indoor championship in its first three years and a record six English Bowling Association (EBA) singles titles between 1960 and 1975 ... Former Tottenham Hotspur and England soccer player **Glenn Hoddle** was born in **1957.** He played for England 53 times. After a spell in French football, he returned to England and went into management with Swindon Town guiding them to the Premier Division in 1993. He then took charge at Chelsea ... In **1962** Australian swimmer **Dawn Fraser** became the first woman to swim 100 metres in under one minute when she clocked a time of 59·9 seconds ... A crowd of 54,569 watched the **Great Britain rugby league team beat Australia 19–12** at Wembley in **1990.** It is the biggest crowd recorded at a rugby league international outside Australia.

**28** Irish snooker player **Dennis Taylor** was born in **1949.** Snooker fans will long remember his marathon match with Steve Davis in the final of the 1985 Embassy World Championship at the Crucible Theatre in Sheffield. The last frame took 68 minutes to complete and was one of the most nail-biting climaxes imaginable, Taylor winning the game with the last black and ending the suspense for an estimated $18\frac{1}{2}$ million BBC television viewers ... Rugby player **John Bevan** was born in **1950**. He played rugby union for Cardiff, Wales and the British Lions before turning professional with Warrington in 1973. He then won Wales and Great Britain honours at the 13-a-side code ... **Georges Carpentier,** one of the most versatile of all boxing champions, died in **1975** at the age of 81. By the age of 19 he held European titles at welterweight, middleweight, light-heavyweight and heavyweight. He was world light-heavyweight champion between 1920 and 1922, and also challenged unsuccessfully for the world middle- and heavyweight titles.

**29**

**Wilfred Rhodes,** the oldest man to play Test cricket, was born on this day in **1877.** Yorkshire-born Rhodes was 52 years and 156 days when he played for the last time, against West Indies at Kingston, Jamaica, in April 1930. In 58 Tests for England he scored 2235 runs and took 127 wickets ... **Muhammad Ali** (then known as Cassius Clay) won his first professional fight in **1960** in his home-town of Louisville, Kentucky, beating Tunney Hunsaker on points over 6 rounds. Ali won 56 of his 61 professional fights, 37 by knockout ... On this day in **1985** jockey **Lester Piggott** rode one winner at Nottingham before going into retirement. However, training winners was not the same as riding them and in 1990, aged 54, Piggott made a successful comeback ... **Colin McMillan** became the fastest outright winner of a Lonsdale Belt when he won his third British title fight as a featherweight in **1991** against Sean Murphy. He had won his first fight in the division on 22 May, only 160 days earlier.

**30** A crowd of 68,029 was attracted to the second division game between **Aston Villa and Coventry City** on this day in **1937,** the highest attendance recorded at a ground to watch a League game outside the top division of the League ... One of the world's finest footballer-cum-'handball' players, **Diego Maradona,** was born in **1960.** He made his debut for Argentina at the age of 17. He led Argentina to their second triumph in the World Cup in 1986 after a controversial win over England in the quarter-finals. A blatant hand ball, which he later poetically described as 'the hand of God', helped Argentina on their way to the final, although his second goal in the match against England was one of sheer magic. Multi-million pound transfers took Maradona from South America to Barcelona, Napoli and then, in 1992, to Seville who sacked him a year later ... Fourteen years and one day after making his professional debut, **Muhammad Ali** became the second man after Floyd Patterson to regain the world heavyweight title when he knocked out George Foreman in the eighth round of their contest at Kinshasa, Zaïre, in **1974.**

**31** Australian snooker player **Eddie Charlton** was born in **1929.** Known as 'Steadie Eddie' because of his deliberate style of play he was one of the leading players in the 1970s and early 1980s. He later earned himself a reputation as a television summarizer. An all-round sportsman in his younger days, Charlton was a fine boxer; a member of the crew that won the Australian surfing championship; an above-average cricketer; good at roller-skating and athletics, and a senior grade Aussie rules footballer for many years. In addition, he was one of the torch-bearers of the Olympic flame when the Games went to Melbourne in 1956 . . . Cyclist **Jeannie Longo** of France was born in **1958.** She has won a record eight individual world titles and was the Women's Tour de France champion between 1987 and 1989 . . . In **1987 Chetan Sharma** of India became the first cricketer to perform a hat-trick in the World Cup when he dismissed three New Zealand batsmen at Nagpur.

# NOVEMBER

**1**

**Airdrieonians beat Dundee Wanderers 15–1** in a Scottish League second division game in **1894** to record the biggest win in British League soccer ... South Africa's finest golfer, **Gary Player,** was born in **1935.** An outstanding golfer who stayed at the top for more than 20 years, he won his first major tournament, the British Open, in 1959 and his last, the US Masters, at the age of 42 in 1978. He is one of only four men—Gene Sarazen, Ben Hogan and Jack Nicklaus are the others—to win golf's four Majors ... The popular **BBC radio programme** *Sports Report* first went on the air in **1947.** Over the years it has had many famous front men, including Eamon Andrews and Desmond Lynam ... Top British swimmer **Sharron Davies** was born in **1962.** She won the silver medal in the 400 metres individual medley at the Moscow Olympics in 1980 ... Manchester United and Wales striker **Mark Hughes** was born in **1963.** A prolific goalscorer, Hughes played for Barcelona and Bayern Munich before making a much welcomed return to Old Trafford in 1988 ... **New Zealand** established a world record score for a rugby international when they won 106–4 against Japan at Tokyo in **1987.** The puzzle is how Japan managed to score four points.

**2**

Australian tennis player **Ken Rosewall** was born in **1934.** He won the Australian, French and US titles but never Wimbledon, despite contesting four finals there between 1954 and 1974. In the 1974 final he was soundly beaten 6–1, 6–1, 6–4 by Jimmy Connors, who was only two years of age when Rosewall appeared in his first Wimbledon final ... Moroccan long-distance runner **Said Aouita** was born in **1959.** In 1983 he held world records at four recognized IAAF distances: 1000, 2000, 3000 and 5000 metres. He won the 5000 metres at the Los Angeles Olympics in 1984 and at the World Championships in 1987.

**3** Australian tennis player **Roy Emerson** was born in **1936.** Emerson won the Wimbledon title twice, in 1964 and 1965, both times at the expense of fellow Australian Fred Stolle. He won more major titles than any other male player, his total of 28 included 12 in singles ... **Gerd Müller,** the most prolific goalscorer in World Cup history, was born on this day in **1945.** Müller scored a record 14 goals for West Germany in the World Cup competitions of 1970 and 1974 ... Boxer **Larry Holmes** was born in **1949.** He won the world heavyweight title in 1978, beating Ken Norton on points over 15 rounds. He made 20 successful defences before losing to Michael Spinks in 1985 and suffering his first defeat in 49 professional fights; had he won, Holmes would have equalled Rocky Marciano's record ... Arsenal and England striker **Ian Wright** was born in **1963.** He joined Arsenal from Crystal Palace for £2·5 million in 1991 and has proved himself to be one of the most lethal strikers in English soccer ... In **1990 Simon Hodgkinson** scored 23 points for England against Argentina at Twickenham to beat Douglas Lambert's 79-year-old record by one.

**4** On this day in **1886** champion jockey **Fred Archer** had his last ride in public, aboard Tommy Tittlemouse in the Castle Selling Plate at Lewes. Four days later Archer committed suicide (*see 11 January and 8 November*) ... **David O'Leary** played his 622nd game for Arsenal's first team in **1989,** a club record. Sadly, the game against Norwich at Highbury produced some of the most disgraceful scenes of the football season. Most of the players became involved in a brawl after Arsenal were awarded a penalty in injury-time. Arsenal scored from the spot and ran out 4–3 winners (*see 27 November*) ... **Bryan Robson** announced his retirement from international football after being left out of the England squad for the game against Poland in **1991.** He made 90 appearances for England.

**5**

Arsenal manager **Herbert Chapman** persuaded London Transport to change the name of the proposed new underground station close to Highbury from Gillespie Road to Arsenal on this day in **1932** ... Jockey **Lester Piggott** was born in **1935.** Lester comes from a family with a great racing tradition: his great-grandfather Tom Cannon rode 13 Classic winners, his grandfather Ernest Piggott rode three Grand National winners, and his father Keith trained Ayala to win the 1963 National. Lester has ridden a record 30 English Classic winners including a record nine Derby winners. Up to the end of the 1992 season he had ridden over 4400 winners in Britain and had also clocked up wins in almost every other racing nation in the world. He was champion jockey on the flat 11 times. Piggott hit a personal low in 1987 when he received a three-year prison sentence for tax evasion ... In **1971 Her Royal Highness Princess Anne** was voted Sportswoman of the Year by the British Sportswriters Association following her win on Doublet in the European Three-Day Event at Burghley ... **Eamon Andrews** died on this day in **1987.** Although better known to TV viewers as the host of *This Is Your Life* and *What's My Line*, he started his career as a boxing commentator and presented sports programmes on both BBC radio and television for many years.

**6** **Mark McCormack,** founder and head of the International Management Group (IMG), was born in **1930.** IMG is the biggest sports management company in the world and controls the interests of top players in many different sports, from tennis to skiing. McCormack hit on the idea of marketing individual sporting talents when an old schoolfriend, Arnold Palmer, began taking the world of golf by storm. Palmer became McCormack's first client and together they helped to promote the game of golf worldwide. McCormack is no mean golfer himself and in his younger days played in both the US and British amateur championships and also in the US Open.

**7** Top three-day eventer **Lucinda Green (née Prior-Palmer)** was born in **1953.** She won the 1982 world championship on Regal Realm, was twice European champion, and won Badminton a record six times between 1973 and 1984 ... England international soccer player **Mark Hateley** was born in **1961.** After playing for Portsmouth and Coventry he went to Italian club AC Milan and then to Monaco in the French league before returning to Britain and joining Rangers. His father, Tony, played for Aston Villa and Liverpool ... Another England footballer, Liverpool's **John Barnes,** was also born on this day, in **1963.** Jamaican-born Barnes started his career with Watford before a £1 million move to Liverpool where he soon became a firm favourite with the Kop ... The former world heavyweight boxing champion **Gene Tunney** died on this day in **1978,** aged 80. Tunney beat Jack Dempsey on points to win the title in 1926 and a year later retained the title with another points win over Dempsey. Tunney retired as the undefeated champion in 1928 (*see 22 and 23 September*) ... Manchester City's **Adcock, Stewart and White** contributed a hat-trick apiece to their team's 10–1 drubbing of Huddersfield town in **1987.** It was only the fifth time that three players had scored hat-tricks in the same Football League game ... In **1991** the Los Angeles Lakers basketball star **'Magic' Johnson** shocked the American nation with the announcement that he was HIV-positive.

**8** Jockey **Fred Archer** died on this day in **1886** from self-inflicted gunshot wounds. The 29-year-old former champion had suffered depression for two years following the death of his wife in childbirth (*see 11 January and 4 November*) ... **Martin Peters,** one of the heroes of England's 1966 World Cup team, was born in **1940.** He started his career with West Ham and then, in 1970, joined Tottenham Hotspur becoming Britain's first £200,000 player. Peters scored one goal in the 1966 World Cup final.

**9** US golfer **Tom Weiskopf** was born in **1942.** Weiskopf won the British Open at Troon in 1973 with a score of 276 which equalled Arnold Palmer's championship best and was not bettered until 1977 when Tom Watson won at Turnberry with a score of 268. Weiskopf won 15 US Tour events, none of them majors ... In **1985 Gary Kasparov** became the youngest world chess champion at 22 years and 210 days when he beat the defending champion Anatoly Karpov in Moscow.

**10** The **BBC televised its first rugby league game** in 1951, an international between England and New Zealand at Swinton ... **Mike Powell,** the man who broke Bob Beamon's 23-year-old world record in the long jump, was born in **1963.** He won the gold medal at the world championship in Tokyo in 1991 with a record leap of 29 feet $4\frac{1}{2}$ inches (10·2 m). In the Barcelona Olympics in 1992, however, Carl Lewis, the defending champion, avenged defeat in the world championships by taking the gold medal and as in Seoul in 1988, Powell had to be content with silver ... **'Sugar' Ray Robinson** announced his retirement from boxing on this day in **1965** after more than 25 years in the professional ring. A month earlier the 44-year-old former world middleweight and welterweight champion had lost on points to Joey Archer in Pittsburgh. Robinson won 175 and drew 6 of his 202 professional fights ... **Henry Cooper** won the European heavyweight title for the third time on this day in **1970** when he stopped José Urtain of Spain in the ninth round. Cooper had relinquished the title the previous year because of injury but still managed to win the title back at the age of 36 ... **Sir Gordon Richards,** one of the greatest and most successful of all British jockeys, died in **1986** at the age of 82 (*see 5 May*) ... **Steve Davis** suffered his biggest defeat in a final in 13 years as a professional when he was beaten 9–1 by Stephen Hendry in the final of the **1989** Duty Free Masters in Dubai.

**11** The **first athletics meeting of any description to be held in the United States** took place indoors at the Empire Skating Rink, New York, in **1868.** The meeting was organized by William B. Curtis who had recently formed the New York

Athletic Club. Curtis introduced spiked shoes at this first meeting ... Belgian moto-cross rider **Joël Robert** was born in **1943.** The most successful moto-cross rider of all-time, Robert won six world titles, all at 250 cc. He won a record 50 races in the 250 cc class between 1964 and 1972 ... **Rodney Marsh,** the most successful wicketkeeper in Test cricket, was born in **1947.** In 96 Test matches for Australia between 1970 and 1984 he dismissed a record 355 victims, 343 of them caught and 12 stumped ... On this day in **1986** Pakistan's **Jahangir Khan** lost his first match since April 1981 when he went down to Ross Norman in the final of the World Open Squash Championship ... In **1990 Monica Seles** beat Gabriela Sabatini 6–4, 5–7, 3–6, 6–4, 6–2 in the final of the Virginia Slims Championship in New York. It was the first five-set match in a major women's event since the 1901 US Championship doubles.

**12**

Romanian gymnast **Nadia Comaneci** was born in **1961.** The star of the 1976 Montreal Olympics, she became the first gymnast in history to score a maximum 10 points in international competition. She followed that with six more maximums and, not surprisingly, won three gold medals, a silver, and a bronze. She won two more golds at the 1980 Olympics and collected 11 world and European championship gold medals. She defected to the West in 1989 ... In **1990** a Football Association disciplinary commission decided to fine **Arsenal and Manchester United** £50,000 each as punishment for the brawl involving 21 players at Old Trafford on 20 October. In addition to the fine, two league points were deducted from Arsenal and one from United (*see 20 October*).

## 13

The **United States** won the first World Contract Bridge Championship in Bermuda in **1950**. The competition, which is held every two years, comprises two events, one for men and the other for women. The winning national side in the men's competition receives the Bermuda Bowl. The women contest the Venice Bowl ... **Sporting Lisbon beat the Cyprus team Apoel Nicosia 16–1** in the first round of the European Cup-winners' Cup in **1963**. It is the biggest score recorded in soccer's three major European club competitions ... **Evander Holyfield** lost his world heavyweight title to Riddick Bowe in Las Vegas in **1992** after two years as champion.

## 14

England fast bowler **Harold Larwood** was born in **1904**. Larwood was the bowler at the centre of the famous 'bodyline' controversy during the 1932–33 series in Australia. The Australian captain Bill Woodfull accused the England side of 'not playing cricket' after he had been hit twice by bouncers from Larwood ... French cyclist **Bernard Hinault** was born in **1954**. Hinault won the Tour de France five times between 1978 and 1985 to equal the records of Jacques Anquetil and Eddy Merckx ... Another top cyclist, Japan's **Koichi Nakano,** who was born in **1955,** shares Hinault's birthday. Nakano won the world professional sprint title every year from 1977 to 1986 ... **Bobby Moore** bowed out of international soccer on this day in **1973** with an appearance for England, his 108th, against Italy at Wembley. The home side lost 1–0 ... The former Manchester United assistant manager **Jimmy Murphy** died in **1989** at the age of 79. Murphy took charge of the United team in the aftermath of the Munich air crash. Murphy missed the game in

Belgrade because he was on duty with Wales for a special World Cup qualifier against Israel. By rights the Welsh team should not have been playing because they had been eliminated from the competition. Israel, however, had won their qualifying group by a walkover because of a political boycott by their opponents. FIFA ruled they could not go to the World Cup finals without playing a match. Consequently, the runners-up from the other groups, including Wales, were put into a draw to decide which of them should play Israel. Wales came out of the hat and Murphy was saved from experiencing that tragic crash at Munich. Wales won the match 2–0.

**15** In **1952** goalkeeper **Ted Sagar** played his 463rd and last League game for Everton, against Plymouth. His playing career with Everton lasted 22 years and 10 months and is the longest association between a player and a club in the history of the Football League ... The **Liverpool versus West Ham** game in **1969** was the first football match to be shown in colour on BBC's *Match of the Day.* Liverpool won 2–0 ... The **Australian Grand Prix** in Adelaide formed a round of the world motor-racing championship for the first time in **1987.** The race was won by Austria's Gerhard Berger ... **Nigel Martyn** became the first £1 million goalkeeper in Britain when he moved from Bristol Rovers to Crystal Palace in **1989.**

**16** In **1938** Tottenham's **Willie Hall** scored three goals in $3\frac{1}{2}$ minutes against Ireland in Manchester, a record in a 'home international'. Hall scored two more goals in England's 7–0 win ... Jockey **Willie Carson** was born in Scotland in **1942.** Willie is one of only five jockeys with over 3000 winners in Britain to his name. He has won all the Classics, including Derby victories in 1979 and 1980, on Troy and Henbit respectively. He was champion jockey five times between 1972 and 1983 and also appeared for a time on BBC television's *A Question of Sport* as Bill Beaumont's opposing captain . . . British heavyweight boxer **Frank Bruno** was born in **1961.** Probably the second most popular British boxer after Henry Cooper, Frank has had two attempts at the world title, losing in 11 rounds to Tim Witherspoon in 1986 and in five rounds to Mike Tyson in 1989.

**17** One of the first greats of women's golf in Britain, **Joyce Wethered,** was born in **1901.** She won five consecutive English championships (1920–24) and the British Open four times between 1922 and 1929. Bobby Jones once described her swing as 'one of the best ever'. She became Lady Heathcoate-Amory on her marriage to Sir John Amory . . . Austrian skiier **Toni Sailer** was born in **1935.** He was the first man to scoop all three golds in his sport at one Olympics, the 1956 Winter Games in Cortina where he won the downhill, slalom and giant slalom (*see 17 February*) . . . The top East German swimmer **Roland Matthes** was born in **1950.** He won the 100 and 200 metres backstroke at both the 1968 and 1972 Olympics. He set 17 backstroke world records between 1967 and 1973 . . . Australian-born rugby league player **Lionel Cooper** scored a British record ten tries for Huddersfield against Keighley in **1951** . . . **Pete Sampras** beat Jim Courier to win the **1991** ATP Championship in Frankfurt for the second successive year and collect a cheque for $625,000.

**18** Welsh golfer **Brian Huggett** was born in **1936.** He won many of the top European Opens and the British Match-Play and Dunlop Masters titles. A member of five Ryder Cup teams, he played in the famous tied match of 1969, holing a 5-foot (1·5 m) putt on the 18th to halve his match with Billy Casper . . . **Joe Baker** made his debut for England against Northern Ireland at Wembley in **1959** and made history as the first player from outside the English Football League to be picked for the national side; he played for Hibernian in the Scottish League at the time. Baker contributed one goal to England's 2–1 win . . . **Fred Daly,** the only Irish golfer to win the British Open, died in **1990** at the age of 79. Daly, a former Ryder Cup player, won the Open at Hoylake in 1947.

**19** With floodlit matches increasingly common, the **white football** was given the seal of approval by the FA on this day in **1951.** Arsenal manager Herbert Chapman had first introduced the white ball in the 1930s . . . **Pelé** scored the 1000th goal of his career during a game for his club Santos against Vasco da Gama in **1969.** The goal, a penalty, was greeted with jubilation all round the ground—the Vasco da Gama goalkeeper peeled off his jersey to reveal a shirt which bore a message congratulating Pelé on his achievement!

**20** **Wilf Wooller,** cricketer and rugby union international, was born in **1912.** He played rugby union for Wales 18 times before concentrating on a career in cricket begun while he was at Cambridge University. A useful all-rounder, he was appointed captain of Glamorgan in 1947. The following year he guided them to their first county championship title, a rare success for the Welsh county ... South African golfer **Bobby Locke** was born in **1917.** Distinguishable in his plus fours and white cap, he first won the British Open at Sandwich in 1949. He retained it the following year and won again in 1952 and 1957. He died in 1988 ... The **shortest British title fight** on record took place at Nottingham in **1961.** Defending lightweight champion Dave Charnley knocked out 'Darkie' Hughes after just 40 seconds of the first round of their title fight ... In **1971 Ted MacDougall** scored nine goals for Bournemouth in the first round of the FA Cup against Margate, the most scored by a player in the competition proper ... In **1977 Walter Payton** of the Chicago Bears rushed for an NFL single game record 275 yards (251 m) against the Minnesota Vikings ... A record **15 football players** from English clubs were sent off on this day in **1982,** twelve in FA Cup games and three in league matches.

**21**

The world's greatest canoeist, **Gert Fredriksson,** was born in **1919.** Swedish-born Fredriksson won a record six Olympic gold medals between 1948 and 1960. In addition, he won one silver and one bronze medal to bring his total to a record eight ... In **1990** 250–1 chance **Equinoctal** won at Kelso to confound the bookies and go into the record books as the longest shot ever to win a horse race in Britain.

**22**

The **National Hockey League** (NHL) was formed in Montreal in **1917** ... Spare a thought for **Billy Minter** of St Albans City. On this day in **1922,** he scored seven goals in an FA Cup tie against Dulwich Hamlet, but still ended up on the losing side. Dulwich won 8–7! ... **Clapton Orient played Brentford** in a Football League game on this day in **1930.** It was the first of only two Football League games (excluding the present-day end-of-season play-offs) ever played at Wembley Stadium ... One of the finest women tennis players of all time, **Billie-Jean King,** was born in **1943.** She won a record 20 Wimbledon titles, including the singles six times between 1966 and 1975. She won her first title as Billie-Jean Moffitt in 1961 when she partnered Karen Hantze to victory in the women's doubles. In 1977 Martina Navratilova helped her to win her 20th and last title, also in the doubles. King won 223 of the 262 matches she played at Wimbledon. Her 71 tournament victories include 12 Grand Slam singles titles and 27 Grand Slam doubles and mixed doubles titles ... German tennis player **Boris Becker** was born in **1967.** He won the Wimbledon title in 1985 and was the youngest-ever men's champion, at 17 years and seven months. He retained his title in 1986 and won the singles again in 1989, the year of his first US Open title. He has won over $12 million in prize-money in his career ... **Mike Tyson** became the youngest world heavyweight boxing champion in **1986** when he beat Trevor Berbick for the WBC title at Las Vegas. Tyson was 20 years and six months old at the time, virtually 18 months younger than the previous youngest champion, Floyd Patterson (*see 11 February* and *26 March*).

**23** | **Thomas Lord,** the man who gave cricket the Lord's Ground, was born in **1755.** He developed his first ground in 1787 before moving to a second site at North Bank in 1809, and in 1814 to the present-day site at St John's Wood ... Australian tennis champion **Lew Hoad** was born in **1934.** He won the Wimbledon title in 1956—the year he completed three legs of the Grand Slam— and 1957. The US title was the one to elude him in 1956, fellow Australian Ken Rosewall beating him in the final ... Another top Australian sport personality has a birthday on this day: swimmer **Shane Gould,** who was born in **1956.** She won three gold medals at the 1972 Olympics: in the 200 and 400 metres freestyle, and the 200 metres individual medley. Between January 1971 and January 1972 she set world records in all five internationally recognized freestyle distances, from 100 to 1500 metres. She retired in 1973 at the age of 16!

**24**

Three former England Test cricketers were born on this day. **Herbert Sutcliffe,** one of England and Yorkshire's most prolific batsmen in pre-war days, was born in **1894.** He scored 4555 runs in his 54 appearances for England. He is one of only seven batsmen to score over 50,000 runs in first-class games, between 1919 and 1945. On three occasions he scored 3000 runs in a season. Sutcliffe died in 1978 at the age of 83 ... **Ken Barrington,** a member of the successful Surrey team of the 1950s, was born in **1930.** He appeared in 82 Tests and scored 6806 runs at an average of 58·67. He died in Barbados in 1981 ... **Ian Botham** was born in **1955.** He made his first-class debut for Somerset in 1974. A great all-rounder, he was the first player to make 3000 runs and take 300 wickets in Test cricket. He played for England 102 times and captained the side in 12 Tests in 1980 and 1981. In his Test career he has scored 5200 runs, taken a one-time record 383 wickets and held 120 catches.

## 25

Baseball star **Joe DiMaggio,** who led the Yankees to nine World Series titles, was born in **1914.** He hit safely in 56 consecutive games in 1941, an all-time record. He retired in 1951 but came back into the limelight in January 1954 when he married Marilyn Monroe. Nine months later Monroe sued for divorce ... The former England rugby international **Dickie Jeeps** was born in **1931.** He played for England 24 times and went on three Lions tours. He later became chairman of the Sports Council ... Pakistan cricketer, and part-time heartthrob, **Imran Khan** was born in **1952.** He made his Test debut in 1971 and became Pakistan's most prolific wicket-taker with 362 victims to his credit. In 1983 he emulated Ian Botham's record of scoring a century and taking ten wickets in a Test match ... In **1953** the **England** football team was beaten at Wembley by continental opposition for the first time in its history. England were out-played by a Hungarian side brimming with flair and technical skill. The visitors won 6–3 with Nandor Hidgekuti scoring a hat-trick and their captain, the legendary Ferenc Puskas, two beautifully judged goals ... **Peter Shilton** made his debut as England's goalkeeper in a 3–1 win over East Germany at Wembley in **1970.** He kept goal a record 125 times for England and had his last game for the national side in 1990 (*see 7 July*) ... **Australia beat England** by 10 wickets in the first Test at Brisbane in **1990.** The match was completed on the third day, giving Australia their first win over England in three days since 1938.

**26** Rugby league star **Joe Lydon** was born in Wigan in **1963.** He made his name as a winger and centre with the Cheshire club Widnes, collecting a Premiership winner's medal in his first season (1982–83) and a Challenge Cup winner's medal the following season. He won the coveted Lance Todd Award for his performance in the final of the Challenge Cup, which included two tries, from 70 (64 m) and 85 yards (78 m), to set up the win against Wigan. In the same season, 1983–84, he won the Man of Steel (Player of the Year) award. He later moved to Wigan, his hometown team, where he continued to add to his silverware collection.

**27** In **1971 Sammy Chapman** ended Nottingham Forest FC's proud 32-year-old record of not having a player sent off. He was given his marching orders in a game against Leeds United ... Three weeks after the brawl at Highbury in **1989** (*see 4 November*) the FA imposed heavy fines on both **Arsenal** (£20,000) and **Norwich City** (£50,000) in the hope of preventing a recurrence of an incident described as '30 seconds of madness' (*see 20 October*).

**28** Australian Test cricketer **Keith Miller** was born in **1919.** In 55 Tests he scored 2958 runs and took 170 wickets ... In **1929 Ernie Nevers** scored an NFL record 40 points in a single game for Chicago Cardinals against the Chicago Bears. He also scored an NFL record six touchdowns in the game. The Cardinals won 40–6 ... **Dwight Davis,** the man who gave the Davis Cup to lawn tennis, died in **1945** aged 66 (*see 5 July*) ... The former England striker **Mick Channon** was born in **1948.** One of the most popular England players in the 1970s, Channon made his name at Southampton before moving north to Manchester City. He later returned to the south coast club before subsequent moves to Bristol Rovers, Norwich and Portsmouth. He scored 20 goals in the 46 games he played for England between 1972 and 1977. He was the first division's top scorer in the 1973–74 season, but even his goal-scoring talents could not save Southampton from relegation ... **Stephen Roche,** the first Irishman to win the Tour de France, was born in **1959.** He won the gruelling race in 1987, a great season for Roche in which he also won the Tour of Italy and the world professional road race title ... Two games involving first division sides produced 17 goals in the fourth round of the Football League (Rumbelows) Cup in **1990.** High-flyers **Arsenal** were stunned **6–2** at **Highbury** by **Manchester United** for whom Lee Sharpe scored a hat-trick. **Coventry scored five goals** at Highfield Road against **Nottingham Forest** to win a nine-goal thriller and inflict Forest's first defeat in 22 matches in the competition.

## 29

In **1897 Charles Jarrott,** riding a Fournier, won the first ever motorcycle race around a track, at Sheen House, Richmond, Surrey ... One of English rugby union's most prolific kickers, **Dusty Hare,** was born in **1952.** The former Nottingham and Leicester player scored a record 7337 points during his 19-year career, between 1971 and 1989. He scored a then-record 240 points in 25 matches for England ... Manchester United and Wales footballer **Ryan Giggs** was born in **1973.** He is the most exciting player to wear a United shirt since George Best. He made his international debut for Wales against Germany in

1991 aged only 17 years and 321 days, the youngest person ever to play for the country. He was the PFA Young Player of the Year in both 1992 and 1993 . . . British racing driver **Graham Hill** was killed on this day in **1975** when the light aircraft he was piloting crashed onto Arkley golf course near Elstree in Hertfordshire. Also killed was Tony Brise, a promising young driver who was to spearhead Hill's new Embassy racing team (*see 15 February*).

## 30

**England and Scotland** played out a goalless draw at Hamilton Crescent, Glasgow, in the first-ever soccer international in **1872**. The two sides did not produce their next 0–0 score-line until 98 years later . . . **Floodlights** were used in a football international in Britain for the first time, for the last 15 minutes of England's match against Spain at Wembley in **1955** . . . In **1956** 21-year-old **Floyd Patterson** beat Archie Moore for the vacant world heavyweight title to become the youngest world heavyweight champion. Mike Tyson has since become the youngest champion (*see 22 November*) . . . England footballer **Gary Lineker** was born in **1960.** Lineker scored 48 goals for England, just one short of Bobby Charlton's all-time record. He moved to Japan in 1992 to join the Grampus Eight club . . . The **United States beat Norway 2–1** in **1991** to win the first women's soccer World Cup in China.

# DECEMBER

**1** Lee Trevino, one of the great characters of golf, has a birthday today. Of Mexican descent, Trevino was born in Dallas in **1939.** He won the US Open twice, the British Open twice and the US PGA title twice. The US Masters title eluded him, although he came close to winning it several times. In 1971 he won the US Open, Canadian Open and British Open, all within a month ... On this day in **1973 Jack Nicklaus** became the first golfer to win $2 million in prize-money on the US Tour. Nicklaus was also the first to win $3, $4 and $5 million ... The **Medway Bears beat the Richmond Raiders 48–1** in **1985,** a record score in the British Ice Hockey League. In the same second-division match, Canadian-born Kevin McNaught scored an individual record 25 points ... In **1991** the **French Davis Cup** team, skippered by Yannick Noah, beat the United States 3–1 in Lyon to win the tournament for the first time since 1932. The victory caused such a stir in France that the team was honoured at a reception held by President François Mitterand at the Elysée Palace in Paris.

**2** The **Football Players' and Trainers' Union** was formed on this day in **1907.** Earlier attempts, in 1893 and 1898, to form a footballers' union were unsuccessful. The organization became affiliated to the TUC in 1908 and in 1958 changed its name to the Professional Footballers' Association, or PFA ... Defending world bantamweight champion **Vic Toweel** put challenger Danny O'Sullivan on the canvas a record 14 times during their title fight in Johannesburg in **1950;** no world title fight has produced more knockdowns. Toweel stopped his opponent for good in the 11th round ... Yugoslav tennis ace **Monica Seles**

was born in **1973**. She became the world's No. 1 in 1991 after winning the Australian, French and US titles; she did not play at Wimbledon. In 1990, aged 16, she won the French title to become the youngest winner of a Grand Slam title this century.

**3** The **longest bare-knuckle contest on record** took place at Dalesford, New South Wales, in **1855**. The match, between James Kelly and Jonathan Smith, lasted 6 hours and 15 minutes ... The former Kent and England wicketkeeper **Les Ames** was born in **1905**. He claimed 1121 victims at the stumps between 1926 and 1951. Ames was also the most prolific run-scoring wicketkeeper English cricket has seen, with a first-class career total of 37,248 runs to his name; 3058 of these were scored in 1938. Ames died in 1990, aged 84 ... Another England cricketer, **Trevor Bailey,** was also born on this day, but in **1923**. A great all-rounder, Bailey performed the double of 1000 runs and 100 wickets in a season eight times in his career. In 1959 he scored 2000 runs and took 100 wickets ... Ireland's most-capped rugby union player, **Mike Gibson,** was born in **1942**. He won a record 69 caps between 1964 and 1979. He was also capped twelve times by the Lions ... **Franz Klammer,** one of the greatest downhill skiers of all time, was born in **1953**. He won a record 35 World Cup downhill races between 1974 and 1985 and was five times the World Cup downhill champion. He also won the downhill at the 1976 Winter Olympics in Innsbruck ... German figure-skater **Katerina Witt** was born in **1965**. Four times the world champion, in 1984, 1985, 1987 and 1988, she took the Olympic title in 1984 and 1988. She also won six consecutive European titles.

**4** British three-day eventer **Richard Meade** was born in **1938**. A member of the gold medal winning British team at the Mexico Olympics in 1968, he struck gold twice at the 1972 Munich Games, in the individual and the team three-day event. No other British sportsman has won more gold medals ... In **1948** MCC batsman **Denis Compton** scored 300 runs in 181 minutes, the fastest triple century in first-class cricket, against Northern Transvaal ... Ukrainian pole-vaulter **Sergey Bubka** was born in **1963**. The first man to clear 20 feet (6.09 m) both indoors and outdoors, he has set more than 30 world records. He has been world champion three times, in 1983, 1987 and 1991, and in 1988 he won Olympic gold. He went to the 1992 Games in Barcelona a hot favourite to collect gold, but failed to register a height.

**5** The **first rules of Association Football** were published in *Bell's Life* on this day in **1863** ... A first-division football match between **Sunderland and Newcastle United** in **1908** pepped up considerably in the last 28 minutes with Sunderland scoring eight goals and running out 9–1 winners. Their last five goals came in the final eight minutes of the game ... **England beat Australia** by a Test cricket record 675 runs at Brisbane in **1928**. The innings scores were England 521 all out (Hendren 169) and 342–8 declared, and Australia 122 (Larwood 6–32) and 66 all out (White 4–7) ... The first-division football match between **Newcastle United and Portsmouth** at St James's Park in **1931** made history by ending without producing one corner kick. Hardly surprisingly, the final score was 0–0! ... American golfer **Lanny Wadkins** was born in **1949**. He has earned more than $6 million from some 20 tournament wins since turning professional in 1971. His only Major was the 1977 PGA Championship ... In **1960** Southampton's **Derek Reeves** became the first man to score five goals in a Football League Cup match, against Leeds United. His record was equalled but not bettered until 1989 when Frankie Bunn of Oldham scored six (*see 25 October*).

**6**

The former Lancashire and England cricketer **Cyril Washbrook** was born in **1914**. In a first-class career, which lasted from 1933 to 1964, he scored 34,101 runs at an average of 42·67 per innings. He played in 37 Tests and regularly partnered Len Hutton to open for England ... Only 462 spectators turned up at the third-division (south) game between **Thames and Luton Town** in **1930**. This stood as the record for the lowest attendance of a football league match under normal conditions until 1974, when the Rochdale–Cambridge United game drew a crowd of 450.

**7**

**Martin Pipe,** the National Hunt trainer, saddled the 1000th winner of his career at Kempton Park in **1990**. His total of 230 winners in that season earned more than £1 million in prize-money, a record for a National Hunt trainer ... In **1990** the **Scarborough versus Wrexham** Football League game at Seamer Road, Scarborough, attracted just 625, the smallest crowd ever to watch a fourth-division match.

**8** In **1863** at Wadhurst, Kent, **Tom King** of London beat John C. Heenan of the United States in the first boxing match (bare-knuckle) for which a world title (and a $5000 side bet) was at stake ... In **1940** the **Chicago Bears** established an NFL record score of 73–0—which still stands—against the Washington Redskins ... **Geoff Hurst,** the only man to score three goals in a World Cup final, was born in **1941.** He spent most of his career at West Ham United but finished it with spells at Stoke City and then West Bromwich Albion. He scored 24 goals in 49 appearances for England. His only other hat-trick for England was against France in 1969. He now runs a successful car insurance company, along with his former England and West Ham colleague Martin Peters ... Manchester United and Scotland footballer **Brian McClair** was born in **1963.** He started his career at Motherwell after failing to find a place with Aston Villa. He joined Celtic and then, in 1987, moved to Manchester United for £850,000. He has scored over 70 goals for United in more than 200 League games and has been an inspiration throughout their quest for League championship glory in 1992 and 1993. McClair has won 26 Scotland caps ... Germany's football captain, **Lothar Matthäus,** became the first official World Footballer of the Year in **1993** following a poll of FIFA coaches. *World Soccer* magazine has run its own such award since 1982, when Paolo Rossi of Juventus was the first recipient.

**9** Billy Bremner, the man who was an integral part of Leeds United's rise to the top of British football in the 1970s, was born in **1942.** A fiery and tough competitor, Bremner was one of the great captains of his era. He played for Scotland 54 times but his international career ended under a cloud after an alleged brawl in Copenhagen while on duty with the national side in 1975. He later went into management; he managed Leeds for a short time but with indifferent results. His most successful spell in management was spent at Doncaster Rovers ... American golfer **Tom Kite** was born in **1949.** In 1990 he became the first golfer to take his career earnings beyond $6 million. In 1992 he was the first to pass $7 million, and in 1993 the first to pass the $8 million mark. In 1992 Kite also shook off the tag 'Best Player Never to win a Major' by winning the US Open at Pebble Beach by two strokes from Jeff Sluman ... The world record streak of 32 consecutive wins by greyhound Ballyregan Bob came to an end in **1986** when his owner George Curtis decided to retire him and put him out to stud. Bob had not lost a race since 25 August 1984.

**10**

**Jahangir Khan,** arguably the finest squash player of all-time, was born in Pakistan in **1963.** Khan won six world Open titles between 1981 and 1988, and ten consecutive British Open titles between 1982 and 1991. Jahangir's father, Roshan, won the British Open title in 1956 and Roshan's cousin, Hashim, won it seven times between 1950 and 1957, his brother, Azam, also won the title four times (1958–61)! ... In **1982 Michael Dokes** won the WBA heavyweight title by stopping the defending champion Mike Weaver after just 63 seconds of their bout at Caesar's Palace, Las Vegas; it is the shortest world heavyweight title fight on record. Dokes became the first man since Sonny Liston 20 years earlier to win the title with a first-round stoppage (*see 25 September*).

**11** The biggest win in the Scottish League this century was recorded in **1937** by second-division side **East Fife,** who beat Edinburgh City 13–2 (*see 1 November*). In the same season East Fife became the only second-division team to win the Scottish FA Cup, beating Kilmarnock 4–2 in a replay . . . The 21 goals produced in a National Hockey League match between the **Edmonton Oilers and Chicago Black Hawks** in **1985** equalled a 65-year-old NHL record for the highest scoring game. Edmonton won the game 12–9 (*see 10 January*).

**12** American boxer **Henry Armstrong,** known as 'Homicide Hank' or 'Perpetual Motion', was born in **1912** (note the birth-date: 12.12.12). He won the world feather-, light-, and welterweight titles and is the only man to hold three world titles simultaneously, albeit only for a month in 1938 (*see 23 October*) . . . Brazilian motor-racing driver **Emerson Fittipaldi** was born in **1946.** He was the youngest-ever world champion when he first took the title, in 1972, at 25 years and 10 months. He won the title for a second time in 1974. He quit racing in 1980 but made a comeback on the Indy car circuit in the United States. In 1989 he became the first non-North American to win the Indianapolis 500 since Graham Hill in 1966 . . . Coincidentally, on Fittipaldi's 13th birthday, in **1959, Bruce McLaren** of New Zealand took the chequered flag in the US Grand Prix at Sebring to become the youngest winner of a grand prix, at the age of 22 years and 104 days. McLaren was killed in an accident in 1970 . . . American tennis player **Tracy Austin** was born in **1962.** She took the professional circuit by storm reaching the semi-finals at Wimbledon in 1979 at the age of 16 after beating Billie-

Jean King in straight sets in the quarters. She was three months short of her 17th birthday when she became the youngest US Open champion in 1979. She won the title again two years later, but these were her only two Grand Slam titles. Back and neck injuries forced her to quit in 1983, but she made a comeback in 1993.

**13** Boxer **Archie Moore** was born on this day but whether in **1913** or **1916** remains a mystery—even he didn't know! The world light-heavyweight champion between 1952 and 1961, he knocked out 145 of his 234 opponents, a record in professional boxing ... In **1942 Stephan Stanis** scored 16 goals, a world record in a senior professional soccer match, for Racing Club Lens against Aubry-Asturies in the French Cup ... Former jump jockey **John Francome** was born in **1952.** Champion jockey seven times, he equalled Stan Mellor's record of riding 1000 National Hunt winners in a career. After retiring he emulated Dick Francis and wrote racing thrillers but not with the same success ... In **1989 Bryan Robson,** wearing an England shirt, scored the fastest goal in a professional football match at Wembley, taking just 38 seconds from the kick-off to slot the ball in the back of the net. England won the game, against Yugoslavia, 2–1 to record their 100th win at Wembley.

**14** **Henri Cochet,** one of the famous 'Four Musketeers' of French tennis (the others were Jean Borotra, René Lacoste and Jacques Brugnon) who dominated the Davis Cup competition in the late 1920s and early 1930s, was born in **1901.** Cochet won four French, two Wimbledon and an Australian title between 1926 and 1932, and eight doubles titles. He was a member of six Davis Cup winning teams ... Arsenal centre-forward **Ted Drake** scored all seven goals in the team's 7–1 win over Aston Villa at Villa Park in **1935.** He was the first player since Jimmy Ross of Preston in 1888 to score seven goals in a first-division game; no player since has equalled, let alone bettered, their feat ... American tennis player **Stan Smith** was born in **1946.** In 1971 he beat Jan Kodes to win the US Open. Runner-up to Australian John Newcombe in the 1971 Wimbledon final, in the following year he defeated Ilie Nastase in a classic five-setter to take the title ... The Test match between **Australia and the West Indies** at Brisbane in **1960** ended with the scores level after five full days and was declared a tie. West Indies scored 453 and 284 and Australia scored 505 and 232. The only other Test to finish in a tie was the game between India and Australia at Madras in 1986.

**15**

The **first Test match played in India** got under way on this day in **1933.** Their opponents, England, captained by Douglas Jardine, won the match by nine wickets and went on to win the series. Remarkably, England did not win another series in India until the 1976–77 Tour, led by Tony Greig ... The former Scottish international striker **Joe Jordan** was born in **1951.** He started his career in Scotland with Morton but was snapped up by Leeds United after only 10 League games. He later played for Manchester United and Italian clubs AC Milan and Verona before returning to Britain and joining first Southampton and then Bristol City. He managed the Bristol club for a time before returning 'home' to Scotland to take over at Hearts until getting the sack in 1993. In 52 games for Scotland Jordan scored 11 goals, including a Scottish record four in the final stages of the World Cup ... **England beat Luxembourg 9–0** in a European Football Championship qualifier in **1982;** at the time it was a record score in the championship (*see 21 December*). The then England manager Bobby Robson had played for England in a World Cup qualifier 22 years earlier when they beat Luxembourg by the same score.

**16**

One of England's finest cricketers, **Sir Jack Hobbs,** was born in **1882.** In a first-class career lasting from 1905 to 1934, Hobbs scored a record 61,237 runs at an average of 50·65; most were for his county, Surrey. He also scored a world record 197 centuries. In 1926 he compiled an innings of 316 not out against Middlesex at Lord's, his highest score in an innings and a record on the ground for almost 75 years; in 1990 Graham Gooch surpassed it with 333 against India. In 61 Test appearances for England Hobbs scored 5410 runs. He was almost 48 when he played his last Test. Knighted in 1953, he died five days after his 81st birthday in 1963 (*see 21 December*) ... After beating fellow American Brad Gilbert in the final of the Compaq Grand Slam Cup in Munich in **1990, Pete Sampras** gave $200,000 of the $2 million in prize-money to charity.

**17**

Playing for Victoria against Queensland at Melbourne in **1927, Bill Ponsford** scored 437 runs to beat his own world record of 429 set nearly five years earlier ... **Ray Wilson,** a member of the England football team that won the World Cup in 1966, was born in **1934.** A full-back, he was responsible for West

Germany's opening goal in the final—though it didn't matter much in the end! He has very little to do with football these days and is an undertaker in Yorkshire ... Australian media magnate **Kerry Packer** was born in **1937.** He turned the world of cricket upside down in 1977 by announcing plans to launch a World Cricket series. Ian Chappell of Australia and Tony Greig of England were signed up to lead the teams which would be composed of the world's best players. Alarmed by the prospect of losing leading players from the Test arena, the authorities threatened to ban from Test cricket all those who joined Packer's circus. Though some players who took part never found favour with the selectors again the circus folded fairly quickly ... New Zealand middle-distance runner **Peter Snell** was born in **1938.** He won the 800 metres at the 1960 Rome Olympics. Four years later, in Tokyo, he retained his title and also won the 1500 metres to become the first and, so far, only post-war athlete to win both events at the same Games. He broke the world mile record held by Herb Elliott in 1962, with a time of 3 minutes 54·4 seconds, and bettered this two years later. Jim Ryun of America is the only athlete since Snell to better *his own* world record for the mile.

**18**

**Championship belts,** now very much part of world boxing, were introduced in **1810** when Tom Cribb, the popular champion bareknuckle boxer, was presented with one after beating Tom Molineaux at Copthall Common, England. The belt was presented by King George III, a keen fan of pugilism ... Top American amateur golfer **Bobby Jones** died in **1971** at the age of 69 after a long illness (*see 17 March*) ... On the same day in

**1971, Stan Mellor** became the first National Hunt jockey to ride 1000 winners when Ouzo crossed the finishing line first at Nottingham.

## 19

**Liverpool** played their first game under new manager Bill Shankly on this day in **1959.** Shankly had been appointed manager a few days earlier after being released by Carlisle United. The new partnership did not get off to a good start, the second-division side losing their match 4–0 at home to Cardiff City in front of 27,291 fans. Shankly's first Liverpool team was: Slater, Molyneux, Moran (later managed the side), Wheeler, White, Campbell (later managed Fulham and Chelsea), Morris, Hunt, Hickson, Melia (the man who guided Brighton to the 1983 FA Cup Final) and A'Court. Shankly would be instrumental in building the Merseyside club into one of the most successful sides in Europe ... **Gary Kasparov** beat fellow Russian Anatoly Karpov in **1987** to retain the world chess title he won in 1985 ... The Arsenal and England defender **Tony Adams** was jailed for nine months, five of them suspended, on this day in **1990** following a drink-driving offence. On the same day that Adams was sent down, the East German and West German international football teams underwent 'reunification', playing as a **United German team,** the first for 40 years, in a friendly international against Switzerland. Germany won 4–0.

## 20

American motor-cycling ace **Freddie Spencer** was born in **1961.** The world 500 cc champion in 1983, he became the first man to win the 250 and 500 cc titles in the same season two years later; all his titles were won on a Honda. His grand prix career was short, lasting only four seasons (1982–85), but in that time he won 27 races ... Yugoslav midfielder **Dejan Savicevic** became the world's costliest footballer in **1991** when he moved to AC Milan from Atlético Madrid for £11·5 million. Under the deal, Savicevic would receive around £7 million over four years.

## 21

**Walter Hagen,** one of golf's most flamboyant characters, was born in **1892.** He helped to popularize the game in the 1920s and played a considerable role in elevating the status of the professional golfer in both the United States and Britain. He won the US PGA title five times, the British Open four times and the US Open twice. His total of 11 majors has been bettered only by Jack Nicklaus. Hagen died in 1969, aged 76 (*see 6 October*) ... Irish golfer **Christy O'Connor** senior was born in **1924.** A veteran of ten Ryder Cup contests between 1955 and 1973, a record, O'Connor came closest to winning a Major in 1965 when he was runner-up to Peter Thomson in the British Open at Birkdale ... British flat-race jockey **Greville Starkey** was born in **1938.** He rode Shirley Heights to victory in the 1978 Epsom and Irish Derbies. He also won the Arc de Triomphe on Star Appeal in 1975 ... US tennis player **Chris Evert** was born in **1954.** She won a one-time world record 157 tournaments, including 18 Grand Slam singles titles. She won her first Wimbledon singles title in 1974, her second in 1976 and her third in 1981; she was also runner-up seven times ... American track star **Florence Griffith Joyner,** better known as 'Flo-Jo', was born in **1959.** The darling of the track at the 1988 Seoul Olympics, she won the 100 and 200 metres gold medals and added a third in the sprint relay. She retired the following year and in 1990 designed the outfits for the Indiana Pacers basketball team! ... Cricketer **Jack Hobbs** died on this day in **1963** (*see 16 December*) ... The **Spanish national soccer side** had one of its most amazing results on this day in **1983.** The team went into a European Championship qualifying match against Malta at Seville needing to win by 11 clear goals to reach the finals. They won 12–1, qualified, and set the record for the highest score in the championship! (*see 15 December*).

**22**

The **first modern-type speedway race** around a short track was held at West Maitland, New South Wales, Australia, on this day in **1923.** The races were organized by a 31-year-old New Zealander, John Hoskins.

**23**

One of the finest welterweight boxing champions, **Barney Ross** (real name Beryl David Rosofsky), was born on this day in **1909.** He took up professional boxing as a means of supporting his family after gunmen killed his father in Chicago. Ross won the world lightweight and junior-welterweight crowns in 1933 by beating Tony Canzoneri. In the following year he beat Jimmy McLarnin on a split points decision for the welterweight title. Ross lost the return with McLarnin on another split decision before regaining the title with a unanimous decision. All three contests between the two men are rated as 'classics'. Ross lost his title to Henry Armstrong in 1938 ... One of Britain's finest golfers, **Henry Cotton,** died on this day in **1987** (*see 26 January*).

## 24

The former England goalkeeper **Frank Swift** was born in **1914.** Swift played 338 League games for Manchester City between 1933 and 1950. A year after making the first team, in 1934, the 19-year-old Swift collected an FA Cup winners' medal; City beat Portsmouth 2–1 in the final at Wembley. He played 19 games for England. Swift was travelling with the 'Busby Babes' as a journalist for the *News of the World* when the aircraft on which they were all travelling crashed at Munich airport in 1958 (*see 6 February*). Swift lost his life in the tragedy . . . England and Kent cricketer **Colin Cowdrey** was born at Bangalore, India, in **1932.** He scored a one-time English record 7624 runs in 114 Test matches between 1954 and 1975. He was the world's first cricketer to appear in 100 Tests; his record of 114 was equalled by David Gower in 1991. Cowdrey and Peter May put on a record 411 runs (the highest partnership by an England pair in a Test match) for the fourth wicket against the West Indies at Edgbaston in 1957. Cowdrey was elected President of the MCC in 1986. His son Chris followed him into both the Kent and England teams.

## 25

The **first game of ice hockey** is believed to have been played at Kingston, Ontario, Canada, on this day in **1855** . . . **Ambrose Brown** of Wrexham will want to forget the football game against Hull City in **1936:** he was dismissed by referee Bert Mee of Mansfield after just 20 seconds. It is the quickest sending off in Football League history. Hull won 1–0.

## 26

The boxing world was horrified when Texan **Jack Johnson** became the first black heavyweight champion of the world in

**1908.** He was not allowed to fight in his native America because of his colour so he travelled to Sydney, Australia, to challenge the Canadian Tommy Burns for the title. The referee stopped the fight in the 14th round after Burns was knocked out for eight seconds ... **Tranmere Rovers and Oldham Athletic** took part in the highest scoring game in Football League history at Prenton Park in **1935.** Tranmere won 13–4. Centre-forward 'Bunny' Bell scored a League record nine goals; his record stood for only four months (*see 13 April*) ... On this day in **1963** a staggering **66 goals** were scored in the first division of the Football League. These are the scores: Blackpool 1 Chelsea 5; Burnley 6 Manchester United 1; Fulham 10 Ipswich Town 1; Leicester City 2 Everton 0; Liverpool 6 Stoke City 1; Nottingham Forest 3 Sheffield United 3; Sheffield Wednesday 3 Bolton Wanderers 0; West Bromwich Albion 4 Tottenham Hotspur 4; West Ham United 2 Blackburn Rovers 8; Wolverhampton Wanderers 3 Aston Villa 3 ... The one-time golden girl of British athletics, **Lillian Board,** died of cancer in **1970** at the age of 22. A silver medallist in the 1968 Olympic 400 metres final, which she lost in the closing strides, she captured the European 800 metres title in Athens the following year ... The **Sheffield 'Derby'** between Wednesday and United at Hillsborough in **1979** drew a crowd of 49,309, the largest at a third-division (now second) match in the Football League.

**27**

**John Charles,** known as football's 'Gentle Giant', was born in **1931.** Superb at either centre-half or centre-forward, he played for Wales 38 times. He scored a one-time record 15 goals for his country. He started his career at Leeds United, making his debut in 1948. In 1957 a big money deal took him to top Italian club Juventus where he spent five seasons before returning to Leeds. He had another spell in Italy, with Roma, before winding up his career at Cardiff City. His brother Mel also played for Wales ... The **Football League programme** on this day in **1949** was watched by a League record 1,269,934 people, an average of 28,862 spectators at each of the 44 games played; this broke the record set only 24 hours earlier, on Boxing Day, when 1,226,098 people attended the matches on offer at grounds round England and Wales. The top attendance was at Villa Park, where 70,000 fans watched the Aston Villa–Wolverhampton Wanderers game. Four games attracted crowds of over 50,000, and in the third division (south) only Aldershot (7318) failed to attract a gate of 12,000 or more ... Birmingham City goalkeeper **Tony Coton** was called upon to face a penalty one and a half minutes into his debut against Sunderland in **1980**. He did his job and saved the spot kick. Birmingham went on to win the match 3–2 ... On this day in **1982** National Hunt trainer **Michael Dickinson** saddled a record 12 winners in a single day.

## 28

**Victoria** completed the highest innings in first-class cricket on this day in **1926** when they scored 1107 against New South Wales at Melbourne. Victoria won by an innings and 656 runs ... The first women's cricket Test, between **Australia and England,** started on this day at Brisbane in **1934** ... In **1990** the readers of an Italian newspaper put Argentine footballer **Diego Maradona** at the top of their list of most hated people, above such worthy candidates as George Bush, Saddam Hussein and Madonna!

**29**

US heavyweight boxer **Jess Willard** was born in Pottawatomie County, Kansas in **1881**. Regarded as the 'Great White Hope' who would take the world heavyweight title from the black champion Jack Johnson, he did just that in 1915. He lost his title to Jack Dempsey four years later after just one defence (*see 5 April*) ... British showjumper **Harvey Smith** was born in **1938**. He won the King George V Cup at the Horse of the Year Show on Mattie Brown in 1970. He caused offence in some quarters, and amusement in others, when he gave an inverted 'V' sign to his critics at the British Showjumping Derby at Hickstead in August 1971. Smith won the event four times in his career ... American jockey **Laffit Pincay junior** was born in **1946**. His career earnings of more than $170 million makes him one of the biggest earning sportsmen of all time ... Rugby league player **Martin Offiah** was born in **1966**. In 1992 he became the game's most expensive player when he moved from Widnes to Wigan for £440,000 (*see 3 January*).

**30**

One of the best-known speedway stars, New Zealand's **Barry Briggs,** was born in **1934**. He won four individual world titles, in 1957, 1958, 1964 and 1966, and appeared in a record 18 finals between 1954 and 1972 ... **Gordon Banks,** probably England's finest-ever goalkeeper, was born in **1937**. He started his career with Chesterfield and then moved to Leicester City and, finally, Stoke City. His career was tragically cut short after he lost an eye in a car accident. He played for England on 73 occasions ... **Chris Chataway** became the first recipient of the *BBC Sports Personality of the Year* award in **1954**. Made annually each December, the winner is the sports personality who receives the most votes from a poll among BBC viewers. The award has the names of all recipients engraved on it ... Top British showjumper **Nick Skelton** was born in **1957.** He set a British highjump record (7 feet $7\frac{1}{4}$ inches/2·3 m) on his horse Everest Lastic in 1978 ... Disgraced Canadian sprinter **Ben Johnson** was born in **1961** (*see 24 September*) ... Former world heavyweight boxing champion **Sonny Liston** died at his home in **1970,** aged 38 (*see 8 May*).

## 31

The former Surrey and England cricket captain **Peter May** was born in **1929.** May later became chairman of the England selectors (*see 24 December*) ... Speed ace **Sir Malcolm Campbell** died on this day in **1948,** aged 63 (*see 4 February and 11 March*) ... The former French rugby union flanker and captain **Jean-Pierre Rives** was born in **1952.** He played for Toulouse and RCF, and represented his country 59 times between 1975 and 1984. He captained the side a record 34 times during that period.